EUCHARIST AS A CELEBRATION OF FORGIVENESS

Eucharist as a Celebration of Forgiveness

Francis J. Moloney, SDB

Paulist Press
New York / Mahwah, NJ

Cover design by Dawn Massa
Book design by Lynn Else

Library of Congress Cataloging-in-Publication Data

Names: Moloney, Francis J., author.
Title: Eucharist as a celebration of forgiveness / Francis J. Moloney, SDB.
Description: Mahwah, NJ : Paulist Press, 2017. | Includes bibliographical references and index.
Identifiers: LCCN 2016030871 (print) | LCCN 2016034291 (ebook) | ISBN 9780809153169 (pbk. : alk. paper) | ISBN 9781587686597 (ebook)
Subjects: LCSH: Lord's Supper—Catholic Church. | Lord's Supper—Biblical teaching. | Lord's Supper—Admission of remarried persons—Catholic Church. | Forgiveness—Religious aspects—Catholic Church. | Catholic Church—Doctrines.
Classification: LCC BX2236 .M65 2017 (print) | LCC BX2236 (ebook) | DDC 234/.163—dc23
LC record available at https://lccn.loc.gov/2016030871

ISBN 978-0-8091-5316-9 (paperback)
ISBN 978-1-58768-659-7 (e-book)

Published by Paulist Press
997 Macarthur Boulevard
Mahwah, New Jersey 07430

www.paulistpress.com

Printed and bound in the
United States of America

For Anthony J. Kelly, CSsR

Contents

Preface

The celebration of the Eucharist is described by *Lumen Gentium* (*LG*), the Dogmatic Constitution on the Church from Vatican II, as "the source and summit of the Christian life" (*LG* 11; see also *Sacrosanctum Concilium* 10). Stated simply, such teaching catches one of the most profound truths of the Christian Tradition, especially as it is understood and lived by Catholic Christians. On the one hand, participation in the eucharistic life of the Church generates an encounter with the crucified and risen Lord Jesus, a nourishment that sets the believer on the way and directs her or him throughout the Christian journey (the source). At the same time, such participation challenges the believer with Jesus's unconditional self-gift in love for others, rendered present at the eucharistic table, as the goal toward which all strive (the summit).

Given the centrality of the Eucharist within the Catholic Christian Tradition, it is understandable that its celebration and the theological and pastoral reflection that surround it have had a complex history. This is not the place to rehearse the history of a meal that began in an encounter with disciples "on the night when he was betrayed" (1 Cor 11:23b) and became a "Tradition": something that was "handed on" from one earliest Christian to another (see v. 23a), incorporated in various foundational "narratives" of the Four Gospels (Mark 14:17–21; Matt 26:20–25; Luke 22:14, 21–23; John 6:51c; 13:21–30) that became part of the Christian Scriptures. Although idealized, Luke reports such table celebrations in the gatherings of the earliest Christian community in Jerusalem in the Acts of the Apostles (Acts 2:46; see also Luke 24:30–31, 35, 41–43). Along with baptism, Eucharist—or the Lord's Table—is regarded by all traditions as a Christian practice that has its beginnings in the life of Jesus.

Eucharistic celebration is documented in the subapostolic writing of the *Didache* 9:1—10:7 (c. 100 CE), Ignatius of Antioch's *Letter to the Ephesians* 20:2 (c. 107 CE; see also 13:1; *Letter to the Philadelphians* 4;

Letter to the Smyrnaens 8:1), and what we might call an "order of service" appears in Justin Martyr's *First Apology* 65–67 (c. 155 CE).[1] These beginnings already indicate a variety of practices by different people in different settings and in different times. For example, the central role of bread and wine, with reference to the saving flesh and blood of Jesus, is clearly stated in Justin's *First Apology* (66). The earlier instruction of the *Didache* first attends to the cup (9:1; see Luke 22:7), but there is no mention of the wine representing the blood of Jesus shed on the cross. Similarly, the broken bread represents its physical origins as wheat scattered over the hills, brought together to become one, as a symbol of the unity of the Church (9:4). There is no mention of the broken body of Jesus. As also reflected in Paul's discussion with the Corinthians about their meal-practices at which some eat and drink in excess (1 Cor 11:17–34), the Lord's Supper in the earliest Church was part of a regular meal. The *Didache* instructs, "After you have had enough, give thanks" (10:1).[2] The uniformity of ritual and theology that is central to today's celebrations was not part of Christianity's eucharistic origins.[3]

Reference to the celebration of the Eucharist and theological reflection on what was called in Latin "the Mysteries" (*Mysteria*) are unfailingly present across the great patristic traditions of East and West. Universally celebrated in Greek, the earliest common language used by the emerging Christian Church (its Sacred Scripture, the New Testament, is in Greek), it developed a Latin form in North Africa, for example, at the Church of St. Augustine (354–430 CE) in Hippo, located in today's Algeria. By 380 CE, it was celebrated in Latin in Rome. This practice gradually spread across the late Roman Empire, and the Latin language remains a crucial formative element in the liturgies of the Roman Catholic form of Christianity. This tradition (perhaps unfortunately) was reinforced by the 2001 document from the Congregation for Worship, *Liturgiam Authenticam*.[4] There are many other cultural and linguistic traditions embodied in eucharistic liturgies reflecting these various origins, and subsequent diverse histories and cultures: Greek, Russian, Ukrainian, Coptic, Chaldean, Melkite, Maronite, and Syro-Malabar, to mention only some of the more ancient traditions. Although it has not had an easy passage since its promulgation in 1963, the Dogmatic Constitution on the Liturgy from Vatican II (*Sacrosanctum Concilium* [*SC*]) affirmed the importance of the inculturation of the Roman liturgy, under the direction of national Episcopal Conferences (*SC* 40).[5] In its manifold forms, wherever and however it is celebrated, the Eucharist has always been the bedrock on which the Catholic Christian Tradition is founded.[6]

Contemporary Catholics have been rightly educated to regard access to the Eucharist as a privilege that flows from their faith in God, and the saving death and resurrection of his Son, Jesus Christ. Over the centuries, the recognition of the treasure of the Eucharist has led to practice (and legislation) that limits access to full eucharistic participation only to those "worthy" of such a privilege. This sentiment has very ancient origins. In 54 CE, Paul warned the Corinthians against eating the bread and drinking the cup "unworthily" (1 Cor 11:27; Greek: *anaxiōs*), and the author of the *Didache* (c. 100 CE) warns, "But let no one eat or drink of your Eucharist except those who have been baptized into the name of the Lord, for the Lord has also spoken concerning this: 'Do not give what is holy to dogs'" (9:5).[7] Some fifty years later, Justin Martyr develops this teaching further: "No one is allowed to partake except one who believes that the things which we teach is true, and has received the washing that is for the forgiveness of sins and for rebirth, and so lives as Christ handed down" (*First Apology* 66).[8] Beginning with these admonitions, directed to specific aspects of "worthiness," we have come, down through the centuries, to the universal requirement that only those without serious sin may participate fully in the Eucharist.

This blanket prohibition has led to the contemporary prohibition of access to the Eucharist to those whose first sacramental marriages in the Catholic Tradition have failed, and who have subsequently remarried. They are automatically regarded as living in a permanently adulterous situation, judged as sinful and thus "unworthy" of admission to a full participation in the Eucharist. Given the complexity of society and the challenge of maintaining lifelong relationships in a sometimes hostile secular world, many bishops and priests have questioned the wisdom of this practice, asking that more understanding and mercy be shown. Pope Francis asked the Church's leadership to consider this matter, side-by-side with many other challenges that face Catholic married and family life, at a significant Synod of Bishops held in October 2014 and October 2015.[9] Pope Francis signed off on his post-synodal exhortation, *Amoris Laetitia*, on March 19, 2016. It is a fine balance of a respect and a restatement of the best of the Catholic Tradition and an unprecedented openness to the complexities of contemporary married life and sexual relationships.[10] Issued during the Holy Year of Mercy (2015–16), the document breathes a fresh air of nonjudgmental pastoral care, based on mercy and forgiveness. It will prove to be a watershed in the history of the Catholic Church's teaching on marriage, family, and human sexuality.

One of the potential problems raised by the current thought and practice of the Catholic Church (in a very broad sense, including the Eastern Churches), especially its discipline, is the conflict with Jesus's eucharistic presence to the Church, as it is presented in the sources of our faith. The stern prohibition of Jesus's eucharistic presence to the "unworthy" is not found in the teaching and practice of Jesus himself and the inspired transmission of that teaching in the Sacred Scriptures of the New Testament. All the accounts of Jesus's final evening with his failed and failing disciples (Mark 14:17–31; Matt 26:20–35; Luke 22:14–34; John 13:1–38) report darkness, betrayal, denial, fear, and flight. Yet he gives himself unconditionally to them in a gesture that is explained by words that only Matthew reports. He adds to Jesus's words over the cup: "This is my blood of the covenant, which is poured out for many *for the forgiveness of sins*" (Matt 26:28). All the narratives insist that failing disciples are gifted with the Lord's presence in the shared wine and the broken bread. But Matthew explicitly raises the question that this book will consider: Is the Eucharist a celebration of forgiveness? If the Eucharist is "the source and summit of the Christian life" (*LG* 11; *SC* 10), does it accompany the Christian on her and his lifelong journey through the challenges of the blessedness and joy of graces received, accompanied by the sinfulness, selfishness, and failure of graces rejected? In other words, as well as providing the essential encounter with the crucified and risen Lord that inspires and nourishes the Christian journey, does it also celebrate the forgiveness of sins, an integral part of the Christian journey?

The current legislation in the Roman Catholic Church is clearly articulated in its *Code of Canon Law* (*CJC*). Two situations are described that call for exclusion from the reception of the Eucharist. The first regards those Catholics who are aware that they are in a situation of grave sin but persevere "obstinately" in that situation; such people "are not to be admitted to holy communion" (*CJC* 915). The most common (but not the only) contemporary situation where this law applies is when Catholic faithful have contracted a second marriage, after the breakdown of a first sacramental union, without receiving an annulment of the initial marriage. The second refers more generically to any situation where a believer is "conscious of grave sin."[11] Such people are reminded that they must make use of the sacrament of reconciliation before going to communion. The Canon reminds the faithful that the possibility of perfect contrition could apply in this situation, when the sacrament of reconciliation is not available (*CJC* 916). Summing this up, the *Catechism of the Catholic Church* states,

> Anyone who desires to receive Christ in Eucharistic communion must be in the state of grace. Anyone aware of having sinned mortally must not receive communion without having received absolution in the sacrament of penance. (no. 1415)[12]

No serious Catholic theologian wishes to deny the holiness and significance of the Eucharist in our Tradition, but a tension between the original revealed witness of the sacrament's place and purpose in the Word of God of the Scriptures, and the current practice described above, is clear. Understanding of the Eucharist as the celebration of forgiveness (see Matt 26:28) has faded from current Catholic thought and practice. Pope Francis is asking the Catholic Church to look again at this teaching, in the light of the Gospel and the authentic Tradition of the Church: "Our teaching on marriage cannot fail to be instructed and transformed by this message of love and tenderness, otherwise, it becomes nothing more than the defence of a dry and lifeless doctrine" (*Amoris Laetitia* 59).

The following chapters attempt to ease that tension by means of four related reflections. The first will look back to the earliest written reflection in the Christian Tradition that deals explicitly with the celebration of the Eucharist, or the Lord's Supper: 1 Corinthians 10:1—11:34. This opening chapter is important for two reasons. First, it forces serious reflection on the essence of the Eucharist: Jesus's self-gift in love "for others" (see 11:24) that must be "remembered." Second, it will lead us to examine the widespread use of 1 Corinthians 11:27–28 outside its Pauline context. The passage, generally cited without context, asks for an act of judgment about who is worthy or unworthy of participation in the eucharistic meal. Over the Christian centuries, 1 Corinthians 11:27–28 has played a major role in limiting access to the

Eucharist to "the worthy," thus lessening the traditional understanding of the Eucharist as a celebration of forgiveness. This traditional use of 1 Corinthians 11:17–34 has been explicitly rejected by Pope Francis in *Amoris Laetitia* (see nos. 185–86).

Pope John XXIII asked the fathers of the Second Vatican Council to return to the sources to reexamine our traditions in order to speak more faithfully to the *contemporary* Church and world in a way that reflects more authentically our *origins*. The analysis of the oldest eucharistic text we have in Paul's Letter to the Corinthians must be followed by a reading of the narratives that appeared in the Gospels of Mark (c. 70 CE), Matthew (late 80s CE), Luke (late 80s CE), and John (c. 100 CE). The process of returning to the sources, so essential to all contemporary theological and pastoral activity in the Church, is described by the widespread use of the self-explanatory French work: *ressourcement*, a return to the sources of our faith. The need for the Catholic Church to initiate a renewal process aided and directed by the process of *ressourcement* is an indication that unhelpful practices, regarded by some as the doctrine of the Church, have gathered across the centuries. They can be questioned by means of closer attention to the sources of Christian life and practice.

Our third reflection will examine the development of the process of exclusion from the eucharistic table. As well as the often misunderstood interpretation of 1 Corinthians 11:27–28, Paul exhorts the elimination of a person in an incestuous relationship from the community in 1 Corinthians 5:1–8. The author of Hebrews 6:1–8 also advocates exclusion from the community. Exclusion was certainly in place in the earliest centuries of the Church's practice, as we have already seen in our citations from the *Didache* (c. 100 CE) and Justin Martyr's *First Apology* (c. 155 CE). This trajectory will then be traced in two figures from the golden era of the fathers of the Church whose ministry was exercised in different locations and circumstances, the Greek-writing Cyril of Alexandria (378–444 CE), and Latin-writing Augustine of Hippo (354–430 CE). The earliest Church saw the need to protect the unity and holiness of the Christian community, and necessarily, the holiness of the sacrament of the Eucharist. What was said by Paul and the fathers of the Church was reinterpreted further in the medieval period, and at the time of the Catholic response to the Protestant Reformation. There has never been a time in the history of the

Church when the eucharistic table was open to whoever might wish to approach it. Criteria for the practice of exclusion were in place from our beginnings, and must remain in place.

The final reflection will attempt to bring together these historical, exegetical, theological, and pastoral considerations. The Christian Tradition of the Eucharist, one of its central and foundational elements, begins with a powerful expression of the gift of the crucified and risen Jesus Christ to fragile and sinful disciples. It explicitly states that one of the purposes for a "new covenant" is "for the forgiveness of sins" (Matt 26:28). Some, no doubt, exclude themselves from such graces, but a case for the Eucharist as a celebration of forgiveness needs development and articulation. Respect for Christian theological and ethical traditions is necessary, and contemporary concern for the divorced and remarried must be attended to, as Pope Francis has requested, and as demanded by the Holy Year of Mercy.

Nevertheless, there can be little doubt that the Eucharist is a crucial presence of a God who forgives in and through his crucified and risen Son. The Church teaches that the Eucharist is both the source and the summit of the Christian life (*LG* 11; *SC* 10). The Word of God prompts us to raise these issues. Writing into the conflictual situation of his Corinthian community, Paul proclaims the following doxology:

> Blessed be the God and Father of our Lord Jesus Christ, the Father of mercies and the God of all consolation who consoles us in all our affliction, so that we may be able to console those who are in any affliction with the consolation with which we ourselves are consoled by God. (2 Cor 1:3–4)

A reflection on the Eucharist as a celebration of forgiveness asks that we take seriously the biblical understanding of the superabundance of God's mercy and consolation showered on the disciples of Jesus, so that we may, in turn, "console those who are in any affliction."

This study is dedicated to my long-standing friend and colleague, the celebrated Australian philosopher, poet, and systematic theologian, Anthony J. Kelly, CSsR. We have worked side-by-side in Australian theological education for fifty years. We basked in the new energies that emerged immediately after the Second Vatican Council, and have grappled with various challenges as the world and the Church we serve have been transformed across that half-century, for better and for worse. I was appointed the Foundation Professor of Theology at Australian Catholic University in 1994. Tony succeeded me in that position in 1999. Although geographically separated by a number of years in other ministries within the broader mission of the Catholic Church, we continued our collaboration. We are proud of a study we coauthored during that time, an attempt to marry a critical exegesis of the Gospel and Letters of John and its concomitant theological possibilities: *The Experience of God in the Johannine Writings.*[13] In 2012, I was invited to return to Australian Catholic University. I again joined forces with Tony in our roles of Senior Professorial Fellows in the Faculty of Theology and Philosophy. Thus, our latter years of teaching and writing have been enriched by sharing the wisdom, and especially the good company, afforded by the philosophical and theological community of Australian Catholic University. Much of what follows reflects Tony's influence, but the mistakes are all mine!

Francis J. Moloney, SDB, AM, FAHA
Australian Catholic University
Melbourne, Victoria, Australia

Abbreviations

AT	Author's Translation
BCE	Before the Common Era (traditionally BC)
CCC	Catechism of the Catholic Church
CE	Common Era (traditionally AD)
CCSL	Corpus Christianorum: Series latina. Turnhout, 1953–
CJC	*Codex Iuris Canonici* (Code of Canon Law)
DS	Henricus Denzinger and Adolfus Schönmetzer. *Encheridion Symbolorum: Definitionum et Declarationum de Rebus Fidei et Morum*. 33rd ed. Freiburg: Herder, 1965.
DV	*Dei Verbum*
LG	*Lumen Gentium*
LXX	Septuagint
NRSV	New Revised Standard Version
NT	New Testament
OT	Old Testament
PG	Patrologia graeca [= Patrologiae cursus completus: Series graeca]. Edited by J.-P. Migne. 162 vols. Paris, 1857–1886.
PL	Patrologia latina [= Patrologiae cursus completus: Series latina]. Edited by J.-P. Migne. 217 vols. Paris, 1844–1864.
RSV	Revised Standard Version
SC	*Sacrosanctum Concilium*

CHAPTER 1

The Eucharistic Teaching of 1 Corinthians 10:1—11:34

"Proclaim the Lord's death until he comes."

(1 Cor 11:26)

The practice of forgiveness is a feature of Christianity. It requires the recognition of sinfulness, repentance, and an active search for pardon. Forgiveness in the Christian Tradition has its roots in the gospel accounts of Jesus's forgiveness of others (see Luke 23:34) and his teaching of the importance of forgiveness among those who claim to be his followers (see Matt 18:23–35; Luke 15:11–32; 24:47–48). The call for repentance also has its origins in the earliest Christian Tradition: "If we confess our sins, he who is faithful and just will forgive us our sins and cleanse us from all unrighteousness" (1 John 1:9; see also Mark 1:4; 4:12; Matt 6:14–15; 7:1–5; Luke 3:3; 6:37; 11:4). The witness of the New Testament Scriptures indicates implicitly and explicitly that the Eucharist was a celebration of forgiveness. As we will see, forgiveness is implied in all four Gospels, as Jesus shares a final meal with those who betray him, deny him, and desert him (Mark 6:17–31; Matt 26:20–35; Luke 22:14–38; John 13:1–38). The association between Eucharist and the celebration of forgiveness is rendered explicit in the words of Jesus over the cup: "poured out for many for the forgiveness of sins" (Matt 26:28).

Despite the close association between Eucharist and forgiveness in the foundation of the Christian Tradition, there is never an understanding of the Eucharist as an encounter with the saving effects of the death and resurrection of Jesus that was open to all who wished to participate, no matter what their situation with others and before God. The earliest Church saw the need to devote attention to those who were permitted access to the eucharistic table. We have already mentioned Paul's instructions on the man in an incestuous relationship in 1 Corinthians 5:1–6, the call for exclusion by the author of the Letter to the Hebrews in 6:1–8, and the concern of the early Church fathers over those who should not be admitted to the Lord's Table.

Given its importance in the development of the Christian eucharistic traditions, the most significant passage from the earliest record of the Church is found in 1 Corinthians 11:27–29. Read without its context, it is an ancient and powerful recommendation that only the worthy be admitted to the eucharistic table:

> Whoever, therefore, eats the bread or drinks the cup of the Lord in an unworthy manner will be answerable for the body and blood of the Lord. Examine yourselves, and only then eat of the bread and drink of the cup. For all who eat and drink without discerning the body, eat and drink judgment against themselves.

Our exercise of *ressourcement* (returning to our origins) must devote careful attention to beginnings. But a warning must be issued. Often these ancient Christian texts have been cited without any reference to their contexts. Original meaning is determined by an original context. For example, as a very trivial but simple example, one could claim that the Bible says, "There is no God." But the whole verse proclaims, "Fools say in their hearts, 'There is no God'" (Ps 14:1). This, of course, is a very simple example of the importance of context, but it shows the crucial importance of what might be called "literary context." Sometimes passages have many contexts: the literary context in which it is found (as in the example of Ps 14:1), the broader literary context of the document in which it is found (e.g., the Book of Psalms as a whole, where God is the very reason for the existence of Israel's prayer). There are contexts of a setting in life, as well as a setting within literature. For example, the context of the living situation within which a given statement or affirmation is made (Israel at prayer), and the context of the audience for whom and to whom a statement is made (a people losing their sense of God). In order to understand our origins properly, we must take seriously the principle that *text without context is pretext*. The later Christian use of biblical texts without devoting careful attention to their contexts sometimes does violence to the original text.[1]

On the basis of a contextualized understanding of widely used texts from the formative years of Christian life and practice, we will be better placed to trace the development of the Christian Tradition that lead to the practice of widespread exclusion of those considered "unworthy" of full participation at the Lord's Table. From the very beginnings of Christianity, an important tradition of reserving the full participation in the Church's eucharistic life to the worthy emerged. But we must attend to what was meant, at the beginnings of our Tradition, by the "worthy" and the "unworthy," further guided by our broader biblical and theological context of the Church's eucharistic life and practice. Is it possible to understand the Eucharist as a celebration of forgiveness, if only those who have no need of forgiveness participate? The traditional response to this, in Catholic circles, was to claim that it was legitimate to attend when conscious of less serious faults (so-called "venial sins"). Many argued that such failures were forgiven at the Eucharist, and that this is what is meant by Matthew's addition of the words "for the forgiveness of sins" to Jesus's words of institution (see Matt 26:28). Even in that situation, communicants were reminded that they were less than perfect and advised that they should seek sacramental Reconciliation as soon as possible.

With these important thoughts on context, we begin our reflection on the Eucharist as a celebration of forgiveness with a study of Paul's discussion of the celebration of the Lord's Table in 1 Corinthians 11:17–34 for two reasons.[2] First, this is our earliest Christian text on the celebration of the Eucharist. Second, reading the passage without careful attention to its literary and theological place within Paul's First Letter to the Corinthians, and especially within its immediate context of 1 Corinthians 8—14, has led to a limitation of Christian participation in the Table of the Lord that does not reflect what Paul was saying to the Corinthians. Above all, for Paul, the celebration of Eucharist was to remind Christians that Jesus gave himself "for others" (see 11:24) and that they, in turn, should match Jesus's way of life, proclaiming the Lord's death until he comes again (see 11:26).

There are very few narratives about the life of Jesus in Paul's Letters. Many critics discuss possible Pauline references to Jesus's words and ministry across his correspondence, but there is a clear use of narrative when he tells the Corinthians of Jesus's final meal with his disciples in 1 Corinthians 11:23–25, and of his death, burial, resurrection, and postresurrection appearances in 15:3–8. He also establishes Jesus's Jewish credentials by insisting in Galatians 4:4 that in the fullness of time he was born of a Jewish woman, under the law. Especially important, in the two passages written to the Corinthians, is Paul's insistence, "For I received from the Lord what I also handed on to you" (1 Cor 11:23; see also 15:3). Paul did not "invent" these narratives. He was one of the earliest Christians, transformed from persecutor to passionate apostle of Jesus Christ in the early 30s CE (see Gal 1:12–16, 13, 23; Phil 3:6; 1 Cor 9:1; 15:8–9). What Paul tells his community about the night Jesus was betrayed (1 Cor 11:23) was something he learned from those who had been part of that darkest night in Christian history: it comes from the Lord Jesus. For this reason, we can claim that in 1 Corinthians 11:23–25, we have our earliest account of the celebration of the Eucharist in extant Christian documents.[3]

There are other explicit narratives dealing with Jesus's final night with his disciples and his institution of the eucharistic meal. We will have occasion to reflect on these narratives, but they were written many years after Paul wrote to the Corinthians (Mark, c. 70 CE; Matthew, late 80s CE; Luke, late 80s CE; and John, c. 100 CE). No doubt drawing on much older traditions and practices with which the early communities were familiar, these accounts are also shot-through with the inspired (and inspiring) theological and pastoral concerns of their authors. There are also accounts of meals celebrated in the Jerusalem Church in the early chapters of the Acts of the Apostles (see Acts 2:42–47; 20:7–11; 27:33–36), but these reports were written by Luke in the 80s and 90s of the first century and are deeply influenced by Luke's understanding of the Christian community and its challenges. Paul's discussion with his Corinthian converts speaks to a very real situation early in the 50s, the first *written witness* to the Christian Tradition of the practice of the Eucharist. Of course, eucharistic life and practice was alive in Christian communities before any written testimony, reaching back to Jesus's meal with his disciples, the night before he died, as Paul informs us (1 Cor 11:23).[4]

Paul's dependence on the eucharistic practices of his Corinthian Christians, however, extends beyond 1 Corinthians 11:17–34, where he deals explicitly with their celebration, citing the words and actions of Jesus on the night he was betrayed (vv. 23–25). Before dealing with that question, he is concerned about their participation at both the Table of the Lord and the pagan cults (10:14–22). His critical point of comparison is the Eucharist: "The cup of blessing that we bless, is it not a common union in the blood of Christ? The bread that we break, is it not a common union in the body of Christ? Because there is one bread, we who are many are one body, for we all partake of the one bread" (10:16–17 AT). The Corinthians have already heard from Paul on the crucial nature of their eucharistic lives by the time he turns to his concerns with the rumor that they think they are celebrating Eucharist, but humiliating those who had nothing (11:17–34).

Paul's attention is directed primarily toward new Christians who were having difficulty in living the Christian life they had accepted. Even though 1 Corinthians 10—11 does not have the full narrative setting of Jesus's gift of himself to his disciples in the Eucharist the night before he died, it is articulated in 11:24 ("This is my body that is for you") and presupposed throughout.[5] Paul's primary concern is to address the reports of so-called abuses that have been drawn to his attention. Among these problems are issues that arise from the Christians' participating in pagan cults, and eating food that has been sacrificed to idols (10:1—11:1). Celebrating Christian cults within a pagan world that had its own cultic life generated problems. Can participation in all or some aspects of the pagan cults that were part of everyday life in Corinth be accepted in a community that celebrates Eucharist? Once he has addressed that question, Paul turns to consider issues that have emerged "internally," that is, within the cultic practices of the Christian community: the issue of head coverings at gatherings for prayer and prophecy (11:2–16) and the celebration of the Lord's Table (vv. 17–34). As one would expect from Paul, even in addressing these practical problems, his concern is always the foundation and driving force of his life and preaching: the saving death and resurrection of Jesus Christ (see Gal 1:10; Phil 3:7–11; Rom 3:21–26). His arguments never move far from his passionate commitment to the fruits of the bloody events that took place on Calvary.

The background setting and context for Paul's use of the earliest witness we have to Jesus's final meal with his disciples is without doubt one that causes concern for Paul over the "worthiness" of the participants, and even over the "worthiness" of the celebration itself (see 1 Cor 11:20: "When you come together, it is not really to eat the Lord's supper"). We must read the Word of God within the Tradition (See *DV* 10, 12), but the primary context for the correct interpretation of 1 Corinthians 11:27–28 must be Paul's First Letter to the Corinthians. The use of critical methods for reaching ancient biblical texts within a Christian community that regards those texts as its Sacred Scripture can sometimes produce a "tension," but that can be a healthy relationship that shows the never-ending dynamism generated by the close relationship between Scripture and Tradition: "Sacred tradition and sacred scripture, then, are bound closely together, and communicate one with the other. Flowing from the same divine wellspring, both of them merge, in a sense, and move towards the same goal" (*DV* 9).[6]

THE CONTEXT OF 1 CORINTHIANS 10—11

Paul's concerns with the Corinthian Church's celebration of the Lord's Table must be located within their overall historical, literary, and theological context.[7] Throughout 1 Corinthians, Paul addresses problems that have arisen in the community at Corinth. There are divisions among members of the Christian community (chap. 1—4, see esp. 1:11), misuse of the body that does not respect the new situation generated by the death and resurrection of Jesus (5:1—6:20), problems concerning sexual relations in marriage (7:1–9), divorce (7:10–16), and changes in social and sexual status (7:17–40). Living in a pagan world, the Corinthian Christians have divided opinions about which food one should or should not eat (chap. 8—9). Some are overconfident in their abilities to judge what is of value or not in joining pagan cultic celebrations, and thus they are offending the scruples of the weak (10:1—11:1).

Having dealt with problems arising from participation in the cultic celebrations of the pagans (chap. 8—10), Paul addresses in chapters 11—14 a series of divisive problems that were arising within the Corinthians' liturgical assemblies: dress (11:2–16), the Lord's Supper (vv. 17–34), and the use and abuse of the gifts of the Spirit (chap. 12—14). Finally, Paul looks to the problem of the resurrection of the body, as it was also causing difficulties and division in this early Christian community (see 15:1–2). Paul writes to a community that he founded, and that he knows well. There are hints that his authority might well be questioned, but he writes to them nonetheless. This problem will emerge more powerfully in his Second Letter to the Corinthians.[8] He hopes that his authority will be accepted there (see chap. 16), and his passion for the "new creation" generated by the death and resurrection of Jesus (see 2 Cor 5:17; Gal 6:15) eliminates any hesitation he may have felt in writing to his Corinthian Church.[9] He certainly addresses very real problems of "worthiness" in this early Christian community's enthusiastic beginnings.

Although Paul moves from one problem to another, dealing with each one in turn, a common theme can be traced through the issues dealt with in 1 Corinthians 8—14. There are some who see themselves as specially gifted in their new found "religion," generated by the "new creation." This leads them to adopt, and subsequently manifest, an attitude of superiority. Some tend to despise, belittle, override, or ridicule the others. Paul reacts to this false "enthusiasm" in order to protect the people who are treated as inferior. This theme occurs, in different ways, across the Pauline Letters, and not only in 1 Corinthians 8—14. As always with Paul, even this is associated with his core message on Jesus's self-gift *for all.* It is classically articulated in Romans 15:1–4:

> We who are strong ought to put up with the failings of the weak, and not to please ourselves. Each of us must please our neighbor for the good purpose of building up the neighbor. For Christ did not please himself; but, as it is written, "The insults of those who insult you have fallen on me."

Rome was not Corinth, and the problems were no doubt very different. Yet Paul's care for the weak is constant, founded on Jesus Christ's taking on the form of a slave so that God might exalt him and that all might recognize his Lordship in the enigma of an exaltation that flows from unconditional self-emptying (see Phil 2:5–11).

Paul deals with the question of eating food that has been sacrificed to idols throughout chapter 8. There are some Corinthian Christians who are strong in faith and rich in knowledge, and they are content to go ahead and eat such meat. They *correctly* claim that idols are meaningless. Paul asks these "strong people" to renounce the liberty that their faith and knowledge, their living in the new freedom made possible by the death and resurrection of Jesus Christ (see Gal 5:1), have given them. Christ also died for "the weak." They must be respected and cared for. To offend them through eating meat that had been produced by a ritual slaughtering would be to offend Christ (see 1 Cor 8:11–12). Paul presents himself as an example to the Corinthians in chapter 9. He has been given great privileges and gifts by God who has called him to be an Apostle, but it would be better for Paul to die rather than insist on privilege. His role is to take the part of the weak, to be a servant: "To the weak I became weak, so that I might win the weak" (9:22). He uses the image of himself as a long-distance runner, not punishing others to attain the victory, but punishing himself (vv. 24–27). This is the Pauline paradigm for the protection and care of the so-called "inferior"—self-oblation—and he later asks the Corinthians to imitate him, as he imitates Jesus Christ (11:1).

The question of those who regard themselves as spiritually superior sharing in food sacrificed to idols is still in Paul's mind as he opens 1 Corinthians 10 by reminding the Corinthians what happened to Israel despite its many privileges as God's people (vv. 1–13). Paul then turns to the specific issue of idol-worship. The "strong" seem to see no problem in their newfound freedom, in taking part in meals that were associated with pagan sacrifices. "The strong" *correctly* regard such sacrifices as senseless. However, this approach can lead to hurtful arrogance, as it pays no attention to "the weak." God is praised by conduct that builds up the whole body, not by the arrogant assertion of one's own strength and knowledge of what is right or wrong (see 10:31–33).

Having dealt with problems that arise over the sharing in the assemblies and the table of the pagans, meals shared *outside* the Christian community, Paul next turns to the community's own assemblies and the Lord's Table. One of the more remarkable features of the newness of Christianity was the place of women in the life and worship of the Church. Paul himself, with reference to a restoration of the original creative plan of God, declares the following:

> As many of you as were baptized into Christ have clothed yourselves with Christ. There is no longer Jew or Greek, there is no longer slave or free, there is no longer male and female; for all of you are one in Christ Jesus. (Gal 3:27–28)[10]

But is it permissible that this should lead some to demonstrate their newfound emancipation by adopting a "manly" pose in the assembly?

Paul does not minimize the right of women to pray and prophesy, but he demands that it be done with humility and decency. Women must remain women (1 Cor 11:2–16).[11] A similar concern for unity and right order is at the heart of 11:17–34, where the eucharistic words of Jesus himself will be called on to remind the wealthy that Jesus died for all (vv. 23–25). As we will see, for Paul, to celebrate Eucharist in an arrogant and superior fashion that discriminated against the poor and the weak is a denial of all that was Christian in the celebration.

The same concern for the more fragile members of the community lies behind the discussions of chapters 12—14, where some more charismatically gifted people seem to be claiming superiority. While there are many gifts, they should never divide the believers (see 12:27–31; 14:26–33). The community must be marked by the quality of its love (see 13:1–13), not its division into the more and the less gifted. In 1 Corinthians 15, Paul returns to the inevitable point of departure for all that he has to say about the performance of the Corinthians, or of any one who claims to be a follower of Jesus Christ: Christ died for our sins, he was buried, and he was raised. This took place as the fulfillment of Scripture (see 1 Cor 15:3–4). "If Christ has not been raised, then our proclamation has been in vain and your faith has been in vain" (v. 14). Some Corinthians seem to believe, and consequently live, as if they were already enjoying the privileges of the risen life. They need to be reminded of the central place of Jesus's death and resurrection. They do not yet live the risen life. That is yet to come (vv. 20–58).

This brief overview of the evolving argument of 1 Corinthians indicates a polarized early Christian community. There were probably a variety of enthusiastic (and "superior") groups, each with its own understanding of its newfound freedom in its own way. The number of different disciplinary interventions that Paul has to make in the two letters to the Corinthians is a good indication of that. Paul's recourse to his understanding of the eucharistic nature of the Christian community founded on the words and deeds of Jesus appears within a broader literary and theological context addressing hurtful divisions that need to be overcome. There is no agreement over the correct approach to idol worship (1 Cor 8—10), their freedom to behave as they like at community services (1 Cor 11), and their use of charismatic gifts (1 Cor 12—14). Within this rhetoric of a Christ-inspired care for the weak, Paul presents the eucharistic table as a place of union, summoning believers to "remember" the story of Jesus's gift of himself for them. How, Paul asks, can the Corinthian community, founded on the preaching of the cross and resurrection (11:23–25; 15:3–8), "remembering" that cross at its eucharistic celebrations, be divided between "the strong" and "the weak," the "haves" and the "have nots"?[12]

Our former selves have been crucified with Christ in the experience of the death of baptism (see Rom 6:3–6; Gal 2:19), but the symbol of the cross, which Paul raises up over against the "old world," has its roots in the bloody reality of the experience of Jesus. Are the Corinthians prepared to live that reality in their lives? This called for respect for the weak, for whom Christ died (1 Cor 8:11), welcoming them at the eucharistic table (11:27–34).[13] They had to understand that no matter what variety of gifts they had been given, all were called to oneness (1 Cor 12), called to a remarkable quality of love (1 Cor 13), so that the quality of their Christianity would bring outsiders to faith (1 Cor 14).

1 CORINTHIANS 10:14–22

As we have seen, 1 Corinthians 8—10 deals with problems that arose among the Corinthian believers because they lived within a pagan environment. The dangers of injuring the weak through an insensitive use of superior knowledge and understanding, in eating meat sacrificed to idols, were dealt with in 8:1–13. Although 9:1–27 concentrates on the experience of Paul himself, it is used as an example for the community (see especially vv. 19–22). Paul often uses this method. It is pointless only to preach. The preached word must be reflected in the life of the preacher. Paul has no hesitation in telling the Corinthians, "Be imitators of me, as I am of Christ" (11:1; see also 4:16–17; 1 Thess 1:6; Gal 1:16, 24; 4:12; Phil 4:9).

In an introductory passage, Paul deals with the disastrous results of the overconfidence of the fathers of Israel (10:1–13). He warns the Corinthians that there is a parallel between the situation of the chosen people, the Israelites in the desert, and that of "the strong" in Corinth. Indeed, writing to a Christian community, he claims that the Israelites ate a "spiritual food" and drank a "spiritual drink" from a "spiritual Rock." The Rock was Christ (vv. 2–4). Paul is drawing a parallel between the experience of Israel, that passed through the waters of a baptism in its passage through the sea (vv. 1–2), to be nourished, in their time in the desert by a spiritual food and drink from the Rock, which was Christ (vv. 3–4). Reading the account of the Exodus through Christian eyes, Paul claims that Israel had been supplied by God with a privileged participation in the benefits of Christ. Despite this privilege, Israel fell. Thus, warns Paul, "So if you think you are standing, watch out that you do not fall" (v. 12).

Having already insinuated baptismal and eucharistic hints into his argument, Paul returns to the question of the pagan rituals, and eating within those contexts. Paul is, in fact, arguing the same case throughout: the threat "the strong" pose to the community as a whole when they *rightly* insist that "no idol in the world really exists" (8:4). The claim of "the strong" that the idol has no existence is a valid slogan; nevertheless, Paul insists that the Corinthians are to "shun the worship of idols" (10:14 RSV). Between his discussion of idols and the experience of Israel in the desert as a warning (10:1–13), he has presented himself as a positive model (9:1–27). He continues to appeal to "the strong," leading to a final request that they adopt a genuinely Christian attitude toward the sensitivities of "the weak": "Do not seek your own advantage, but that of the other" (10:24). In verses 14–22, he makes his case by means of direct reference to the Corinthians' "common union" with the blood and body of Christ.

Paul conducts his argument by first establishing some essential common ground between himself and "the strong." He raises two rhetorical questions beginning with the expression "is it not..." (v. 16). Such a question (formed by the Greek, *ouki...estin*) expects a positive answer. He takes it for granted that the Corinthians will assent to the truth that the cup and the bread that they share in the Eucharist are to be identified with Christ:

> The cup of blessing that we bless, is it not a common union [Greek: *koinōnia*] in the blood of Christ? The bread that we break, is it not a common union [*koinōnia*] in the body of Christ? (10:16 AT)

The NRSV translates the Greek expression *koinōnia* as "sharing," but this does not quite catch the power of the original Greek. It would perhaps be better to translate it as "communion," which would indicate the depth and mutuality of the sharing involved, but that could lead to confusion. Christians have developed the practice, over the centuries, of speaking of "communion" as the practice of receiving the species at the liturgical celebration of the Eucharist. Thus, I have used the clumsy expression "common union" in my translation. Paul shows in verse 17 that he wants to say more than the union that takes place between Christ and the believer implied by our traditional sacramental use of the term "communion."[14]

Having established that the wine and the bread create a union, Paul argues that the union takes place at two levels: "Because there is one bread, we who are many are one body, for we all partake of the same loaf" (v. 17 AT). It is not only that the person sharing the cup and the broken bread establishes a union with Christ. A further union is established through the "partaking" (Greek: *metechein*) of the *same loaf*: the union between all the members of the celebrating community.[15]

> Through sharing in the body and blood of Christ, believers are united with him and with each other. The physical gesture of eating and drinking at the Christian sacred meal has the effect of bringing into being a new Body which is the physical presence of Christ in the world (see 6:15; 8:12; 12:12–27). All are united with Christ through faith and baptism (Gal 3:26–28). The physical gesture of eating and drinking adds a new dimension. Since all share in the one drink which is Christ and in the one bread which is Christ, Christ (to put it very crudely) becomes a possession which all hold in common, and are thereby forged into unity.[16]

Paul is not primarily concerned with teaching the Corinthian community about the meaning of their celebrations of the Eucharist. Such celebrations and their significance are taken for granted as he uses eucharistic traditions as part of his broader argument and plea for union in the community, that the "strong" might care for the "weak." Yet he provides, in passing, a glimpse of an understanding of the eucharistic meal shared by Paul and the Christians at Corinth. The Eucharist is food for "the body." The celebration of the Eucharist maintains and strengthens the union between the believers and Christ, so that they become, together, the community (a body) that belongs to him.

Clearly, Paul and "the strong" have points of agreement in their understanding of the Eucharist. In 1 Corinthians 10:16–17, Paul can base his broader argument on allusions to shared knowledge and belief. On the basis of their shared Tradition, Paul can instruct his early Christian community. Recalling the practice of sharing the food offered as sacrifice in Israel, he reminds "the strong" of the common union (*koinōnia*) that the people offering the sacrifice had with the altar (v. 18). So it is with any food offered, even to the imaginary and worthless pagan idols (vv. 19–20). This enables Paul to make his central point: the act of taking part in a cultic meal established a close connection between the guests themselves and the power to which the victims had been offered (v. 21).

> Paul clarifies for the Corinthians what *koinōnia*, participation in the body and blood of Christ, means from their own familiar experience of their pagan past and their pagan environment. He does not do this to say something new to them, but plainly to convince and win them over by something long familiar.[17]

In objective terms, "the strong" are correct. Paul has no intention of claiming that sacrificed food or pagan idols have any value (v. 19), although he does associate them with demons (vv. 20–21). However, as "the strong" have agreed with Paul concerning their eucharistic celebrations (vv. 16–17), and as they know from Israel's tradition of sacrificing at the altar (v. 18), ritual gestures have both a vertical and a horizontal implication. Paul insists that Christians who shared in the meals celebrated in pagan temples, in conjunction with the pagan sacrifices, were joining in more than a cheap meal! It was not only the food that was consumed. The horizontal "common union" that was generated by the shared table must also be considered. They joined themselves with pagans who believed that idols had a real existence, and in this way associate with the "vertical." Thus, the naïve Christians, in their supposed strength and knowledge, became "partners with demons" (v. 20), generating a "horizontal" breach with their brethren.

In 1 Corinthians 10:21–22, Paul returns to the central importance of the "common union" that was created between Christ and the believer, and the community of believers who shared at the eucharistic table. To share in the cup and the table of the demons, no matter what "the strong" may have thought they were doing subjectively, was a public rupture between themselves and the rest of the community that could destroy the union created at the Table of the Lord, sharing his cup and his bread. "The strong" are thus told that it is impossible to participate at both the pagan tables and the Table of the Lord. As has already been shown in the experience of Israel (vv. 1–13), one must not understand the Christian sacraments of baptism and Eucharist as securing the believer from all possible danger of contamination.

Paul closes his reflection by a sharp reminder of the ultimate authority of the Lord: "Or are we provoking the Lord to jealousy? Are we stronger than he?" (v. 22). He looks back to his warning descriptions of what happened to an arrogant Israel, which prided itself in its privileges. "God was not pleased with most of them" (v. 5; see vv. 1–13).[18] To threaten the "common union" established "vertically" by the Lord between himself and his community, and "horizontally" within the community itself, by exercising one's "superior" understanding and knowledge is unacceptable.

Paul calls on a basic belief that he shared with his Corinthian converts. No matter what their variations on how they thought the Christian life should be lived, Paul was able to remind them that at the Table of the Lord they established a union with Christ and a union among themselves.[19] "In it we receive the body of Christ and, by receiving it, are and show ourselves to be the body of Christ."[20] Sharing other meals, regarding themselves superior to any contamination from such nonsense as idols, demons, and sacrificed foods, the Corinthians broke the union with fellow Christians, essential for the life of "the body," which is the community.

Paul uses the Corinthian community's celebration of the Eucharist to prove his point. He is not instructing his community on the place and significance of its eucharistic celebrations. He takes that instruction for granted. They know it well, and he is calling on that knowledge in support of his argument. On the basis of the Corinthians' understanding of what happens at the eucharistic table, he is able to instruct them on the need to avoid their ritual associations with pagans. The basis of their understanding is their double *koinōnia*: their "common union" with Christ, and their "common union" with one another. With this case established in 10:14–21, Paul addresses another threat to the "common union" (*koinōnia*) in 11:17–34, where he will ask them to examine their worthiness (vv. 27–28).

1 CORINTHIANS 11:17–34

If the Corinthian believers were theoretically in agreement that the cup of blessing that they blessed and the bread that they broke established a *koinōnia* between the Lord and themselves and a *koinōnia* that was the community (10:14–22), the actual celebration of the Lord's Table must be marked by a "common union" at the level of the shared life of the Corinthian Christians. It appears that such was not the case (11:17–34).

Paul's discussion of the Corinthians' problematic participation in the Lord's Supper is approached in the following fashion. He first attacks the nature of their abuse of the eucharistic table in 11:17–22. This is followed by the Pauline version of the eucharistic words (vv. 23–25) with an additional Pauline exhortation (v. 26). Paul then moves to his more theological conclusions and pastoral recommendations (vv. 27–34).[21] The Greek expression translated "whoever, therefore, eats" (Greek: *hōste hos an esthiēi*) of verse 27, that begins the pastoral recommendations, demands that the passage be interpreted in the light of what Paul has written in verses 17–26.[22] What was the "unworthy manner" mentioned in verse 27? Why must believers "examine themselves" (v. 28)? The context of the passage under consideration provides an obvious response to these questions. In verses 17–22, Paul continues to address the problem of division in the community, especially their lack of care for "the weak," as in 10:14—11:1. He expresses his displeasure over the divisions between "those who have" and "those who have not," which seem to have developed since Paul had been with the community: "I hear that there are divisions among you" (v. 18). These divisions are described as follows:

> For when the time comes to eat, each of you goes ahead with your own supper, and one goes hungry and another becomes drunk. What! Do you not have homes to eat and drink in? Or do you show contempt for the church of God [Greek: *tēs ekklēsias tou theou*] and humiliate those who have nothing? What should I say to you? Should I commend you? In this matter I do not commend you! (vv. 21–22)

As is clear in 10:14–22, the Lord's Supper was a common meal: the one body (the community) shared the one bread. But Paul has heard that this has become impossible at Corinth because such divisions had arisen between the wealthy and the humble that no one was concerned about the other. Paul indicates that there are some people who simply do not have enough to eat (v. 22, "the weak"), while there are others who own their own private homes where they could eat and drink at their leisure without creating divisions at the shared Table of the Lord (vv. 22 and 34, "the strong"). It would be better for the wealthy Corinthians to do such lavish eating in their own houses, rather than *pretend* unity. Their behavior, in addition to humiliating the "have nots," shows that they hold true community in contempt. This is the "unworthy manner" of participating in the Eucharist chastised by Paul in the much-abused passage in verse 27, and the reason for the request that such persons should "examine themselves" expressed in verse 28. The situation has been well summarized by C. Kingsley Barrett:

> The rich man's actions are not controlled by love; they therefore amount to contempt not only of the poor, but also of God, who has called into his Church not many wise, not many mighty, not many noble born (1:26). God has accepted the poor man, as he has accepted the man who is weak in faith and conscience (8:9–13; 10:29f.; Rom 14:1, 3f., 10, 13, 15:1, 7); the stronger (whether in human resources or in faith) must accept him too. It is by failure here that the Corinthians profane the sacramental aspect of the supper—not by liturgical error, or by undervaluing it, but by prefixing it to an unbrotherly act.[23]

But the motivation for Paul's intervention is not only to establish good order. There is more at stake. Paul turns to the saving death of Jesus Christ to ground his demands for Christian behavior. As disunity is being created at the Table of the Lord, he calls on the tradition of Jesus's final meal with his disciples, reminding the Corinthians of something they had already learned from him, and which he himself had received (v. 23a), Paul inserts his tradition of the eucharistic words of Jesus.[24] As Paul reports them in 1 Corinthians 11:23–25, they are highlighted by the command, repeated over both the bread and the wine, to perform the action of breaking the bread and sharing the cup "in remembrance of me" (vv. 24 and 25). This twice repeated command may have had its origins in the earliest liturgies, but it is not only a liturgical instruction to ensure the continuity of the practice.

It is not enough to explain *where the words came from*. That question is a valid approach to an ancient text, as it asks important *historical* questions. It is what is called a *diachronic* approach to texts. However, there is a more important question that must be asked as we read these crucial texts within the Christian community today: *What is their significance in the context in which they are now found?* This approach asks theological and pastoral questions of a text, always locating those questions within a credible historical setting. It is called a *synchronic* approach to texts.[25] Synchronically, Paul is challenging his divided community to take seriously the words of Jesus: "You members of the Corinthian Christian community, do this in memory of me." These words are not *only* a reminiscence of the liturgical practices of the earliest Church, inserted very early to ensure the ongoing celebration of the Lord's Supper. What must the Corinthian community do in remembrance of Jesus's broken body and shed blood? Paul's twofold use of this liturgical formula is an important challenge to the Corinthians to shed their petty divisions based on a distinction between those who have more and others who have less. It summons the Corinthians to a deeper appreciation of their being caught up in the mystery of the obedient self-giving death of Jesus Christ for them (v. 24).[26] In celebrating Eucharist, the Corinthians are caught up in the rhythm of a death "for others." The Lord's Table calls them to a deeper appreciation of the eucharistic nature of the Christian life.

To celebrate Eucharist is to commit oneself to a discipleship that "remembers" Jesus, not only in the breaking of the ritual bread and sharing the ritual cup, but also in "imitation" of Jesus, in the ongoing breaking of one's own body and spilling of one's own blood "in remembrance" of Jesus.[27] As Peter Henrici has rightly argued:

> When Jesus thus enjoins on his disciples the task of doing "this" in his remembrance, all his activity is meant—not only his symbolic gesture at the Last Supper (which can and should be ritually repeated) but also his whole sacrificial attitude of delivering himself up to mankind in obedience to the Father.[28]

For this reason, Paul adds, "You proclaim the Lord's death until he comes" (v. 26). The Lord's death is proclaimed in the world in the broken bodies and the spilled blood of a Church of disciples who live the Eucharist that they celebrate, until he comes again.[29] Paul is instructing his divided Corinthian community: "You break your bodies and spill your blood, and thus remember me."[30] While remembering involves gratitude, it is above all an acceptance of the responsibility to prolong the saving mission of Christ.

> Thanks to this clarification made through the liturgy, the whole Christian life becomes an act of worship and proclamation: it "proclaims the death of the Lord until he comes again"—that is, it makes clear the meaning and the source of the eschatological tension that gives shape to the Christian life (cf. 1 Cor. 7 and the letters to the Thessalonians).[31]

Looking back across Paul's intervention in 1 Corinthians 11:17–34, we can see that he first calls for oneness between the wealthy and the less fortunate in verses 17–22. However, the call to unity is not a call to unity for unity's sake. It is a summons motivated by the need for the Corinthian believers "to remember," to practice at the level of life what they proclaim at the level of ritual (vv. 23–25). "'To remember' in the New Testament, signified almost always to recall something or to think about it in such a way that it is expressed in speech or is formative for attitude and action."[32] It is from this immediate context that one encounters the troublesome verses 27–28. Paul's severe words in these verses follow immediately upon his recalling to the memory of the Corinthian community the "rhythm" of the self-giving life of Jesus, through the words that the Corinthians pronounce in their celebrations of the Eucharist (vv. 23–26). He questions them and corrects the division created in the community by their behavior. To continue in their present practice would be to eat the bread and drink the cup "unworthily" (v. 27). They must examine themselves carefully on these issues before approaching the eucharistic meal (v. 28).

In verse 29, Paul further instructs the Corinthians, "For all who eat and drink without discerning the body, eat and drink judgment against themselves." The interpretation of the expression "the body" generates discussion. A traditional Catholic interpretation has seen it as not discerning the eucharistic presence of the body of the Lord.[33] Traditionally, Protestant scholars have seen it as a reference to "the body of Christ," the community as "Church."[34] Interpretations determined by a Reformation agenda no longer have a place, and the most obvious interpretation is that *both* the body of the Lord and the body of the community are meant. "Not to discern the body" is to fail to recognize the Lord's presence in the Eucharist in the sense of the Lord who died for us (see

v. 24: "This is my body that is for you [Greek: *huper hymōn*]"). In the light of what Paul had already said to the Corinthians about "the body" in 10:16–17, the wider context forces us to pay attention to the fact that Paul is particularly concerned that the Corinthians remember that the body of Jesus was given unto death, in obedience to the Father, in love for them—for all of them who form the one body, which is the Church.[35] If the Corinthians ignore certain members of the community in their eucharistic meals, they are failing to discern "the body" of the community itself. They would be proclaiming the presence of the Lord in a way that ran counter to that very "rhythm" of the offering of Christ that they claimed to be "remembering" in their celebration (vv. 24–26). In his sharp criticism of the traditional use of 1 Corinthians 11:17–34, to exclude the "unworthy" from the eucharistic table (*Amoris Laetitia* 185), Pope Francis rightly affirms, "The celebration of the Eucharist thus becomes a constant summons...to open the doors of the family to a greater fellowship with the underprivileged and in this way to receive the sacrament of the eucharistic love that makes us one body" (no. 186).

The Christian is called to repeat the self-gift of Christ in the "memory" celebrated both in cult and in life. Not to celebrate Eucharist in this way is to "eat and drink judgment" upon oneself (v. 29). By not recognizing the sacrificed "body" of Jesus in the Eucharist, believers offend against the "body," which is the Church, called to repeat that sacrifice in their own lives. As in 10:14–22, Paul is using the community's understanding and practice of the Eucharist to correct their practice, asking them to recall the Tradition (v. 23)—and all its implications! "This counsel meant specifically for the Corinthian Christians who are being summoned to reckon with the selflessness of Jesus at the Last Supper and to cope with their questionable conduct."[36] To threaten the common union established by the Lord between himself and his community, and within the community itself, by an arrogant exercising of one's privileges and "strength," is unacceptable and dangerous (vv. 30–31).[37]

> Paul touches on one of the deepest of all mysteries, if indeed it be true that the paradox of human existence is to be found in the fact that human beings are at once individual persons and essentially social beings. Believers in Jesus become more fully themselves and more closely associated with their brothers and sisters, the more intimately united they are with their Savior.[38]

CONCLUSION

Pauline reference to the celebration of the Eucharist within the community at Corinth challenges a divided community to recall that "because there is one bread, we who are many are one body, for we all partake of the one bread" (1 Cor 10:17). In the light of that truth, Paul's warnings of 1 Corinthians 11:27–28 were written to accuse the Corinthian Christians of sinfulness in celebrating eucharistic meals that humiliated "those who have nothing" (11:22). Paul passes on a Tradition, well described by Hans Conzelmann:

> It is eating unfittingly when the Supper of the Lord is treated as one's "own supper." Then one becomes "guilty" inasmuch as the man who celebrates unfittingly sets himself alongside those who kill the Lord instead of proclaiming his death.[39]

This behavior contradicted what was an "agreed position," stated in 10:16–17. Thus, there was a "lie" in the lives of the faithful: they were not proclaiming with their lives what they were celebrating in cult. There was a "contradiction between an early Christian congregation's quarrels and its understanding of itself as an eschatological community of love."[40] Paul's severe intervention at Corinth, correcting an unworthy celebration of a so-called common meal that the "one body" (the Church) celebrated in its sharing of the one bread and the one cup (the Eucharist), initiates a practice in the Christian Church. The Eucharist must be celebrated worthily.

Saint John Chrysostom (c. 349–407), in his homily on Matthew 14:23–24, indicates that the Church did not lose touch with Paul's original teaching on eucharistic "worthiness":

> Do you wish to honor the body of Christ? Then do not allow it to be scorned in its members, in the poor, who have nothing with which to clothe themselves. Do not honor him in church with silk and then neglect him outside when he is cold and naked....What does Christ gain from a sacrificial table full of golden vessels when he dies of hunger in the persons of the poor. (John Chrysostom, *Homeliae in Mattheum* L, 4; PG LVIII, 508–9)

CHAPTER 2

The Gospels

FORGIVENESS AT THE TABLE OF THE LORD

Paul most likely wrote his final letter toward the end of the 50s CE. His intense focus on the saving significance of what God did for humankind in and through Jesus's death and resurrection (see Rom 3:21–26) casts a shadow across everything he wrote. As we have seen, this was certainly the case for his use of the Tradition he had received about the meal Jesus shared on "the night he was betrayed" (1 Cor 11:23). As Jesus had given his body and blood for others (vv. 24–25), all who followed him were to do the same, and in this way, "proclaim the Lord's death until he comes" (v. 26). Paul's instruction of his erring Corinthians community was to draw them back into the unity that was essential for the life of the one body formed by many (the Church), partaking of the one cup of blessing and the one bread (see 10:16–17).

The narrative tradition of the early Church no doubt began at the dawn of Christianity, perhaps as women reported an empty tomb on the first Easter morning. Yet it took some time before these narratives became the written witness and proclamation that we now call the Gospels of Mark, Matthew, Luke, and John.[1] This development is succinctly described by the Evangelist Luke. As he opens his Gospel, he tells Theophilus, to whom he dedicates his Gospel and the Acts of the Apostles (Luke 1:3; Acts 1:1), that there have been "those who from the beginning were eyewitnesses and servants of the word" (Luke 1:2). Their witness has been further reported by "many [who] have undertaken to set down an orderly account of the events that have been fulfilled among us" (v. 1). Luke, a third-generation Christian, represents the next stage: "I too decided, after investigating everything carefully from the very first, to write an orderly account for you, most excellent Theophilus" (v. 3).[2]

Across the four Gospels, two significant narrative locations deal with the earliest Church's teaching on the practice and significance of the celebration of the Table of the Lord: the reports of the multiplication of the loaves and fishes (Mark 6:31–44; 8:1–10; Matt 14:13–21, 15:32–39; Luke 9:10–17; John 6:1–15) and Jesus's final meal with his disciples the night before he died (Mark 14:12–31; Matt 26:17–35; Luke 22:14–38; John 13:1–38). As well as these obvious passages that reflect the early Christian understanding of the Eucharist, it is universally recognized that the walk to Emmaus in the Gospel of Luke (24:13–35) is based on early Christian liturgical practice. The same can be said for the Lukan Jesus's appearance and final meal and commissioning of his disciples (24:36–49).

Drawing on an expression widely used in the interpretation of the Gospel of John, all these narratives must be understood as examples of a "two-level drama."[3] This means that the events reported in the narrative came to the storyteller *from the memory of events from the life of Jesus* (first level), but they are told in stories that appeared many decades after those events took place. These stories (the four Gospels) were written, proclaimed, and even performed *to address those who received the narratives* (second level).[4] As the early Christians addressed by Mark, Matthew, Luke, and John were in different times, situations, and geographical locations, often the telling of the same basic story (the first level) receives different nuances in its retelling (the second level). These nuances enrich our appreciation of the depth and variety of the foundational Christian understanding of the significance of the celebration of the Eucharist at the beginnings of the life of the Church. They also indicate the ongoing significance of the inspired Word of our Sacred Scriptures in the Church today.

A detailed study of these narratives is beyond the scope of these pages,[5] but a reflection on the similarities and differences of each gospel tradition is an important element in a return to the *sources* of our faith (*ressourcement*), better to understand the richness of early Christian eucharistic life and practice that should continue to shape the life and practice of the Church *today*. We must initially consider the six accounts of the multiplication of the loaves and fishes. They contribute in a small way to an understanding of the Eucharist as a celebration of forgiveness. Crucially, however, the accounts of Jesus's meal with his disciples "the night when he was betrayed" (1 Cor 11:23) call for special attention. As the Gospels of Mark and Matthew are almost identical, with only one major addition: Jesus's words over the cup in the Gospel of Matthew (26:28: "for the forgiveness of sins"), they can be considered together. Luke has shaped his account of this final night in the form of a departing discourse that Jesus shares with his disciples, during which a meal takes place (Luke 22:14–38). Jesus's washing the feet and sharing the morsel with his disciples in John 13:1–38, like Luke 22:14–38, is a unique telling of that final evening, showing how and why Jesus loves his own "to the end" (see 13:1). By way of a conclusion, this chapter will reflect on Luke's postresurrection account of the journey to Emmaus and Jesus's subsequent appearance to the disciples in Jerusalem (24:14–49).

THE MULTIPLICATION OF THE LOAVES AND FISHES

THE GOSPELS OF MARK AND MATTHEW

Many similarities exist between Mark's and Matthew's telling of the multiplication of the loaves. In the first place, unlike the Gospels of Luke and John, they each tell of two such events (Mark 6:31–44; 8:1–10; Matt 14:13–21; 15:32–39). Most interpreters recognize that Mark deliberately situates the first miracle in a Jewish location, picking up from the mission of the Twelve in 6:6b–13. There is no agreement amongst commentators that Matthew continues the same storytelling and theological strategy. However, there is good evidence that the same process of an initial Jewish feeding, followed by a Gentile feeding, is continued by Matthew.[6] For the sake of this reflection, we will focus on Mark, giving the Matthean indications where they are called for.

The disciples return to Jesus in Mark 6:30, telling him of everything that they have done and taught. He invites them to come away to a "deserted place" by themselves (v. 31; Matt 14:13), but they are recognized and a large crowd gathers (v. 33; Matt 14:13). They are on the Jewish side of the Lake of Galilee as Jesus has compassion on the crowds, because they are like sheep without a shepherd (v. 34; Matt 14:14, without the reference to the shepherd). This oblique reference to Jesus as the shepherd of a troubled people introduces a number of themes from Psalm 23: "The LORD is my shepherd, I shall not want" (v. 1; see vv. 4–5). The people are commanded to recline on the "green grass" (Mark 6:39; see Ps 23:2; Matt 14:18), and Jesus prepares a table for them (v. 41; see Ps 22:5; Matt 14:19). They eat of their fill (v. 42; see Ps 23:1; Matt 14:20). Other details indicate Mark's intention to make it clear that Jesus nourishes Israel. The gathering of the people into groups of hundreds and fifties (v. 40) recalls groups of the same number at the Exodus (see Exod 18:21–25; Num 31:14; Deut 1:15), and the broken pieces that remain are gathered into twelve baskets (v. 43; Matt 14:20).

The meal itself is made possible by actions of Jesus that reflect the celebration of the Eucharist: "taking" the loaves, "looking up to heaven," "giving thanks," "breaking bread," and "giving" it to the disciples to distribute (v. 41; Matt 14:19). The Greek expression for the gathered "broken pieces" is *ta klasmata*, the expression used in the early Church to refer to the eucharistic species (v. 43; Matt 14:20).[7] The role of the disciples is important. They wish to send the people away to look after themselves (v. 35; Matt 14:15), but Jesus will not allow this to happen. He commands his disciples, "You give them something to eat" (v. 37; Matt 14:16). They become Jesus's ministers in this foretaste of the gift of the eucharistic meal in Israel.

At first glance, Mark 8:1–10 looks like a repetition of 6:31–44 (as Matt 15:32–39 repeats 14:13–21), but closer analysis shows that there are important differences.[8] Jesus is now located on the Gentile side of the lake. After healing the daughter of the Syrophoenician woman, Jesus moves out of Israel into the region of Tyre and Sidon, and then through the Decapolis, a region of Greek cities (see 7:24–31). There he heals another Gentile, moving the crowd to amazement and a suggestion that he might be the fulfillment of Isaiah 35:5: "The eyes of the blind shall be opened, and the ears of the deaf unstopped" (see Mark 7:31–37). Matthew handles this section of his story differently, but the same point is made. After the "little faith" of the disciples (14:22–33), the failure of Israel (15:1–14), and the ignorance of Peter (15:15–20), Jesus turns to the Gentiles in 15:21–28 (curing the daughter of the Canaanite woman) and many "along the sea of Galilee" (with reference to Isa 9:1–2 and "Galilee of the nations"). As in Mark 8:1–10, the second multiplication of the loaves and fishes in Matthew takes place among the Gentiles who glorify the God of Israel (Matt 15:31).

The motivation for his compassion for the gathered crowd is no longer related to Israel's Psalm 23, but because "some of them have come from a great distance" (Mark 8:3; this is not in Matthew). All hints of the psalm, and the gathering in fifties and one hundreds, disappear. Rather than twelve baskets of remnants, the disciples fill seven baskets with the "broken pieces" (*ta klasmata*) (8:8; Matt 15:37). Seven is a traditional Jewish number for "completion," and refers regularly to the Gentiles.[9] The expressions that recall early celebration of Eucharist return: "taking" the loaves, "looking up to heaven," "giving thanks," "breaking bread," and "giving" it to the disciples to distribute (v. 6; Matt 15:36). Only after the miracle does Jesus return to the land of Israel and encounter the Scribes and Pharisees (vv. 10–11; Matt 15:39—16:1).

Written around 70 CE, Mark uses these two parallel accounts to tell the Christian community that Jesus's table was open to all. Matthew, retelling Mark's story in a different setting in the latter half of the 80s CE, has the same message. Jesus involved the disciples, somewhat against their own desires, to feed both Jew and Gentile with a food that he provides from their poverty (a few loaves and fish). At the end of the feedings, the meal is still available to Jews (from the twelve baskets) and to the Gentiles (from the seven baskets). Something of Paul's insistence on the need to avoid all discrimination at the Table of the Lord reappears. It is understandable that the originally Jewish Christian communities of Mark and Matthew, where those who shared table were strictly monitored, would have difficulty in allowing Gentiles to share food with them. This would have become especially important in the community celebrations of the eucharistic table. The resistance of the disciples in the gospel accounts makes that clear. Mark and Matthew ask disciples of all times to overcome that resistance, to open the table to all, as Jesus had done in feeding, through the ministry of his disciples, both Jew (Mark 6:31–44; Matt 14:13–21) and Gentile (Mark 8:1–10; Matt 15:32–39). Mark and Matthew utter Jesus's command to Christian communities of all ages: "You give them something to eat" (Mark 6:37; Matt 14:17).

THE GOSPELS OF LUKE AND JOHN

The tradition of Jesus's multiplication of the loaves and fishes is reported in the Gospels of Luke (9:1–7) and John (6:1–15). Neither Luke nor John uses this account to address the problem in the early

Church of possible exclusion from the Table of the Lord. Luke's focus is on the commissioning and authority of the Twelve "apostles," the founders of the Gentile Churches, to which Luke's audience belongs. He wants to assure them of "the truth concerning the things about which you have been instructed" (Luke 1:4). John's use of the same tradition focuses on Christology. Jesus gives the bread (John 6:11), and he is not a royal messianic prophet (vv. 14–15). The miracle leads to his self-revelation as I AM HE (v. 20 AT), the true bread from heaven (vv. 25–49), whose flesh is to be eaten and blood consumed (vv. 20–58).

These are important matters for a study of the eucharistic teaching of the New Testament, but may be left to one side in our investigation of the theme of forgiveness at the Table of the Lord.[10] While Mark and Matthew use the tradition of the multiplication of the loaves and fishes to address the question of "inclusion" of all at the table, all four Gospels focus on forgiveness when they come to tell of Jesus's final meal with his fragile disciples.

JESUS'S FINAL MEAL WITH HIS DISCIPLES

The Gospels have given the Church three traditional reports of Jesus's final meal with his disciples. As with the account of the bread miracle, Mark (14:22–26) and Matthew (26:26–29) are almost identical, while Luke goes his own way by constructing a "farewell discourse" around the meal (Luke 22:14–38). John's narrative tells of Jesus's washing the feet of the disciples and sharing the morsel (John 13:1–38). All four Evangelists associate their institution narratives with the presence of Jesus with his failing disciples and the forgiveness of sin.

LAST SUPPER IN MARK AND MATTHEW

The broader setting of Jesus's final meal with his disciples in Mark and Matthew is striking.[11] The passion narrative opens with the description of a plot concocted by the Jewish leaders (Mark 14:1–2; Matt 26:3–5) and is followed by ten further incidents that move from Jesus's words and actions to the words and actions of the disciples. The former is inevitably a report of failure among the disciples (marked A), while the latter manifests Jesus's response to the will of his Father (marked

B). In the section of the passion narrative dedicated to Jesus's final evening with his disciples (Mark 14:1–72; Matt 26:3–75), there are thus eleven scenes. In the sixth of these scenes, set in the midst of the threat of death and the universal failure of the disciples, Jesus shares a meal with his disciples who will betray him, deny him, and desert him. The passage unfolds as a carefully designed literary piece, moving from darkness to light, dominated by the central scene of the Last Supper.

A: The plot (*failure*): (Mark 14:1–2; Matt 26:3–5).
  B: The anointing *of Jesus* (Mark 14:3–9; Matt 26:6–13).
A: Judas joins the plot (*failure*): (Mark 14:10–11; Matt 26:14–16).
  B: *Jesus* instructs the disciples on the preparation of the meal (Mark 14:12–16; Matt 26:17–19).
A: Prediction of Judas's betrayal (*failure*) (Mark 14:17–21; Matt 26:20–25).
  B: Jesus shares the supper with the Twelve (Mark 14:22–25; Matt 26:26–30).
A: Prediction of Peter's denials and the flight of the disciples (*failure*) (Mark 14:26–31; Matt 26:31–35).
  B: *Jesus* at Gethsemane, and the disciples with him (Mark 14:32–42; Matt 26:36–46).
A: Judas's betrayal leads to Jesus's arrest and the disciples flee (*failure*) (Mark 14:43–52; Matt 26:47–56).
  B: *Jesus, Messiah, Son of God, and Son of Man* at the Jewish trial (Mark 14:53–65; Matt 26:57–68).
A: Peter's denials (*failure*) (Mark 14:66–72; Matt 26:69–74).

This literary juxtapositioning of the failure of the disciples, and Jesus's steady movement toward the cross throws into stark relief the wonder of Jesus sharing a meal with the disciples. Indeed, taking episodes 5–7, the centerpiece of the eleven scenes in Mark 14:17–31 (Matt 26:20–35), the account of Jesus's sharing bread and wine with his disciples (vv. 22–25) is framed by Jesus's foretelling Judas's betrayal (vv. 17–21), the denials of Peter, and the flight of all the other disciples (vv. 26–31).[12] For simplicity, what follows makes reference to the Markan text, but a parallel is always found in Matthew.

In the first section of the passage, the beginning of the frame (14:17–21), Mark paints in details that indicate that Judas, who will betray Jesus, belongs to the inner circle of his friends. Jesus "came with the twelve," a group that was especially appointed in 3:14 "to be with him" in a unique way (v. 17). The setting for Jesus's prediction of his betrayal is the meal table, a place sacred among friends. Jesus deepens this theme further as he comments that the betrayer will be "one who is eating with me" (v. 18). In response to the puzzled queries of his disciples (v. 19), the sense of a broken intimacy is intensified by the words of Jesus that link Judas with the group of "the Twelve" commissioned "to be with him" (3:14): "It is one of the twelve, one who is dipping bread into the bowl with me" (14:20). Jesus is to be betrayed by a person who has shared the most intimate of experiences with him. A similar attention to the closeness that exists between Jesus and his future betrayers is found in the other section of the frame devoted to the rest of the disciples (14:26–31). There, Jesus predicts that they "will all become deserters" (v. 27). He uses the image of the shepherd and his sheep (v. 27), but his predictions lead to profound expressions of love and devotion. Peter swears an unfailing loyalty, better than all the others who may desert Jesus (v. 29). He even claims that he is prepared to lay down his life out of loyalty and love for his master (v. 31). Mark adds, "And all of them said the same" (v. 31). These men from Jesus's most intimate circle will prove to be the ones who deny, betray, and desert him.

The Markan (and Matthean) version of Jesus's last meal with disciples who will betray and abandon him is at the center of the passage (14:22–26; Matt 26:26–29). If anything, Matthew *heightens* this message in his minor reworking of Mark's version. The theme of table fellowship with failing disciples opens the passage: "While they were eating, he took a loaf of bread, and after blessing it he broke it, gave it *to them*, and said, 'Take...'" (v. 22). This theme is continued in the sharing of the cup, where the same recipients are again specified: "Then he took a cup, and after giving thanks he gave it *to them*, and all of them drank from it" (v. 23). There is a bond between Jesus and the disciples that Jesus does not abandon: all eat the bread broken (v. 22), all drink of the cup (v. 23), and all sing a hymn together (v. 26). Although neither Mark nor Matthew have the words "for you" in their reporting of Jesus's words over the bread broken (as do Luke [22:19] and Paul [1 Cor 11:24]) or the cup shared (as does Paul [1 Cor 11:25]), there is an intimate dialogue set up between Jesus and the disciples around the table. He commands them, "Take" (14:22), and they do.[13]

The words over the bread and the cup point to the Cross: a body given in death and blood poured out as the result of a body broken (vv. 22 and 24). They point to something beyond the day of crucifixion. The blood is to be a covenant, "poured out for many" (v. 24), and Jesus comments that he will not "drink again of the fruit of the vine *until* that day when I drink it new in the kingdom of God" (v. 25 RSV). The word "until" has a temporal function in the sentence that forces the reader to look beyond the events of the crucifixion. Both the blood poured out for many and the drinking of it again in the kingdom look well beyond Good Friday. Jesus's words, in the midst of predictions of betrayal, flight, and denial, ring out a message of trust and hope. Matthew heightens this message to failing disciples: "I will never again drink of this fruit of the vine until that day when I drink it new *with you* in my Father's kingdom" (26:29).

A body is given and blood poured out to set up a new covenant reaching beyond the cross into the definitive establishment of the kingdom. A covenant with whom, and what sort of covenant? At this point, Matthew adds words to the Markan account to explain the covenant established: "[the] blood of the covenant, which is poured out for many for the forgiveness of sins" (Matt 26:28). The original Markan and Matthean communities and all subsequent Christian communities, Jew and Gentile, are aware that the body broken and the blood poured out have set up a new covenant. In the absence of a clarification in the Markan text, Matthew has made explicit what was implicit in the other traditions: the new covenant presupposes the forgiveness of sins. All other words over the cup make reference to the covenant (see Mark 14:24; Luke 22:20; 1 Cor 11:25), but only Matthew has words on the lips of Jesus that speak of a covenant "for the forgiveness of sins." These words recall Jeremiah 31:34 and Isaiah 53:10–12.[14] A variety of aspects and understandings of the bond between God and his people can be found in the Bible. They generally reflect the situation in which the nation found itself, both politically and religiously.[15] The prophets, who call a sinful people, summoning them to conversion and repentance, "incorporate the language of truth into their message of restoration and covenant renewal that will follow the people's repentance and recommitment to their relationship with YHWH."[16] Matthew, with his well-known concern to relate Jesus with the promises of the Old Testament, recalls the prophets' promise of a covenant for the forgiveness of sins. This addition sheds light on all the accounts of Jesus's final night with the disciples who betray him, deny him, and forsake him. "The passages in Matthew that summon to the forgiveness of sins (18:21–22; 23–35; cf. 6:12) receive their depths from the Lord's Supper. To forgive others their guilt is to participate in the mission of Jesus and reflect the gift received from him."[17]

Across two thousand years of Christian history, the Gospels of Mark and Matthew have proclaimed a covenanted kingdom, thanks to the original presence of Jesus to failing disciples, the first recipients of the bread and the cup. The fundamental significance of their account of Jesus's final meal with his disciples is the establishment of a community that is united to Jesus in a special way. Through the gift that the Master makes of himself, the disciples enter into a close contact with him: "until that day when I drink it new with you in my Father's kingdom" (Matt 26:29; see Mark 14:25). Mark and Matthew have provided an inspired account of Jesus's gift of himself unto death to establish a new covenant for the forgiveness of sins. He established a lasting kingdom with the disciples who frame the narrative of the meal: a betrayer, a denier, and people who will forsake him. The meal that Jesus shared was not a meal for "the worthy." It was a meal for those who were closest to Jesus but who, faced with the challenge to love him even unto death, betrayed, denied, and forsook their Lord. A new covenant for the forgiveness of sins is established in the gift of his body and blood.

THE LAST SUPPER IN LUKE

The Gospel of Luke contains an account of the disciples' last meal with Jesus (22:14–38) that is strikingly different from that of Mark 14:17–31 and Matthew 26:14–35. The supper recorded in Luke 22:14–38 climaxes a long series of suppers throughout the Gospel. These suppers are consistently marked by Jesus's questioning the status quo. He shares the table with sinners; he radically questions the Pharisees on the numerous occasions where he is reported to have been invited to dine with them (see 5:27–32, eating with tax collectors and sinners; 7:26–50, anointing by the sinful woman; 11:37–54, denouncing the Pharisees and the Lawyers; 14:1–24, healing the man with dropsy; and 19:1–8, Zacchaeus). He sets his famous parables on "finding the lost" at table with sinners (15:1–32).

Jerome Neyrey has commented on the function of Jesus's shared meals within the Lukan narrative strategy:

> Jesus' inclusive table fellowship mirrors the inclusive character of the Lukan Church: Gentiles, prostitutes, tax collectors, sinners, as well as the blind, lame, maimed and the poor are welcome at his table and in his covenant.[18]

This Gospel permits no illusions about the composition of the Church of Jesus Christ. It is not made up of "perfect people." Luke understands "the broken" gathering at the Table of the Lord more broadly and more boldly than Mark and Matthew. It is not a question of Gentile and Jew sharing a table founded on disciples who had failed Jesus. Originally told in a largely Gentile Church, Luke's Jesus-story has little interest in those questions. The third Gospel goes to some lengths to show that there are many ways in which one can be considered an "outsider." Indeed, for Luke, they are specially blessed (see 6:20–23). There are those who are guilty of sin, like the prostitute and the tax collector, and there are Pharisees who suffer from their self-righteousness. There are disciples who fail Jesus through the weakness of their faith, and there are members of the twelve who deny him (Peter) and who betray him (Judas). Finally, there are the Gentiles, the materially poor, and the physically maimed people from the highways and the byways who are all welcomed at the table of Jesus.[19]

The theme of Jesus's presence to the broken and the sinful throughout the Gospel reaches its high point at the Last Supper. "This final meal on the feast of Passover crowns the meals, both everyday and festive, which he has taken with his disciples and with sinners during his earthly life."[20] The theme of meals celebrated by Jesus is continued into the Last Meal. Mark and Matthew use a pattern of alternating the actions of Jesus and the failure of the disciples in telling the story of the last moments of Jesus's presence to his failing disciples. There is something of this alternation in Luke 22:14–38:

A. Verses 14–18: The sharing of the first cup and the promise of the fulfillment of the kingdom (*positive*).
  B. Verses 19–23: The account of the meal and the prediction of the betrayal by Judas (*negative*).
A. Verses 24–30: The role the disciples will play in the kingdom (*positive*).

B. Verses 31–34: The prayer of Jesus for Peter, along with the prophecy that he will deny Jesus (*negative*).

A. Verses 35–38: The difficulties that will confront the disciples in their future mission (*positive*).[21]

The similarities with Mark and Matthew, however, come from the fact that Luke is reporting the same event. It retains all the traditional elements of the tragedy and the splendor of the Last Supper. Nevertheless, the dominant feature of its literary shape has been determined by Luke's desire to show that it was also a "farewell discourse."

The Lukan report of the Last Supper is *not only* a narrative about a shared meal *but also* a final discourse. The deliberate use of this widely recognized literary form indicates that while the early Christian Tradition of the Last Supper is being recalled, a unique literary form is utilized.[22] This literary form does not override the essential message of Jesus's presence to his disciples revealed across all the New Testament accounts of the final meal. The form of a final testament, associated with the tradition of Jesus's unfailing presence to his fragile disciples, produces a narrative that is testamentary in literary form, but it is not *only* a final testament.[23] Luke's major focus is on Jesus's commissioning of the Twelve, the founders of the Gentile mission.

In Mark and Matthew, Jesus's words and actions with the bread and wine at the final meal formed the centerpiece of the passage. This is not the case in the Gospel of Luke, as they are associated with the prophecy of the betrayal of Judas (22:19–23). Luke 22:14–38 is not *primarily* about Jesus's eucharistic words, but the last testimony that Jesus left his disciples, within the context of a parting meal. As Paul Minear has commented, "In this story the center of gravity lies not in the words of institution but, as at earlier tables, in the four key dialogues between Jesus and the disciples."[24]

The practice of placing a "farewell speech" on the lips of a great man as he goes to his death is a reasonably common practice in many religious writings from the first three centuries of the Christian era. It is particularly widespread in the biblical literature.[25] In the Old Testament, we find farewell speeches in Genesis 47—50 (Jacob), in Joshua 23—24 (Joshua), and in Deuteronomy 31—34 (Moses). In fact, the whole of the Book of Deuteronomy can be regarded as Moses's farewell speech. In the New Testament, Paul gives a farewell speech at Miletus (Acts 20:17–35), and Peter is portrayed as giving a farewell speech

(2 Pet 1:12–15). Jesus delivers a form of a farewell speech in Luke 22:14–38, and John 14:1—16:33. There is considerable interest on the part of New Testament scholars in a series of Jewish testamentary texts where this technique is used, especially *The Testaments of the Twelve Patriarchs*, which has its origins in the second century BCE, modeled on Jacob's last words in Genesis 49.[26]

The main features of a farewell speech find correspondence in Luke 24:14–38. The Lukan report of Jesus's last meal with his disciples, as well as being a development of the tradition of Jesus's final meal with his disciples, can also be seen as a good example of four basic elements of a final discourse.

1. Prediction of Death

The speech is understood by one who is about to depart, as his "farewell" to his disciples. Thus, there is some indication or prediction of his oncoming death in all of the testaments. In some cases, the death is unexpected (*Testament of Levi* 1:2; *Testament of Naphtali* 1:2–4; *Testament of Asher* 1:2). This prediction serves as the occasion for the speech. *In the Lukan Last Supper discourse*, this is found in 22:15: "I have earnestly desired to eat this passover with you before I suffer," and in 22:22: "For the Son of Man goes as it has been determined" (RSV). Earlier references to the future suffering, death, and resurrection of the Son of Man (9:22, 44; 18:31–33) leave no doubt in the audience's mind that a departure through death is imminent.

2. Predictions of Future Attacks on the Dying Leader's Disciples

One of the fundamental motivations for a farewell speech is to forewarn disciples that they are in imminent danger. Most of the testaments portray this imminent danger as a sign of the end time. *In the Lukan Last Supper discourse*, this feature is found in 22:32–34: "I have prayed for you that your faith may not fail; and when you have turned again, strengthen your brethren....I tell you, Peter, the cock will not crow this day, until you three times deny that you know me" (RSV). It is also present in 22:36: "Now, let him who has a purse take it, and likewise a bag. And let him who has no sword sell his mantle and buy one" (RSV). Here we find the blending of the Gospel tradition concerning the denials of Peter and its use as a warning in the testament.

3. An Exhortation to Ideal Behavior

The testaments devote much attention to the difficulties to be endured in the future. They are to be met with a behavior that will both protect the members of the group from danger, and help them overcome their difficulties. *In the Lukan Last Supper discourse*, the intrusion of the Gospel's final supper theme of Jesus's presence to failing disciples appears strongly. These failing disciples are the object of Jesus's testamentary exhortation. The Last Supper tradition and the testamentary form blend. The instruction to ideal behavior of the "farewell discourse" is found within the context of disciples who squabble (22:24). The exhortation then follows in verses 25–26:

> The kings of the Gentiles exercise lordship over them; and those in authority over them are called benefactors. But not so with you; rather let the greatest among you become as the youngest, and the leader as one who serves. (RSV; see vv. 24–27)

4. A Final Commission

Instructions are given to the disciples concerning their reconstitution after his departure. *In the Lukan Last Supper discourse*, the blending of the traditional theme of Jesus's presence to the sinful at the meal table again intrudes, as it is within the context of a future denial that Peter is commissioned (vv. 33–34). Even though the commission is delivered to failing disciples, it still stands. The apostles are to continue what he has left with them, even after his departure. This is found in Luke 22:31–32: "Simon, Simon, behold Satan demanded to have you, that he might sift you like wheat, but I have prayed for you that your faith may not fail; and when you have turned again, strengthen your brethren."[27]

The Lukan use of the theme of the meal has served to show that Jesus shared his Last Supper with broken disciples, while the use of the literary form of a farewell discourse establishes them as his legitimate successors (see also Luke 9:1–10). Luke's narrative blends the essential elements of the Last Supper tradition with the literary pattern of a farewell speech. By intermingling both, Luke has been able to continue the tradition found in Mark and Matthew: the presence of Jesus to disciples who betray, deny, and desert. But he has also been able to reinforce an important truth in the Gentile settling of the Lukan Church: the disciples and apostles are the legitimate successors of Jesus of Nazareth, however sinful they may have been.

The disciples are instructed and commissioned in the midst of failure (see especially vv. 31–38). Luke has produced a singular example of the farewell discourse form. Jesus's disciples, despite the brokenness of their table fellowship with the Lord, are also the apostles, the ones who will continue his presence, preaching repentance and forgiveness of sins "to all nations" (24:47; Acts 1:8). This theme continues into the Acts of the Apostles. At a crucial moment, as Peter responds to the promptings of God to preach Jesus to the Gentiles, he announces to the household of Cornelius:

> God raised him on the third day and allowed him to appear, not to all the people but to us who were chosen by God as witnesses, and who ate and drank with him after he rose from the dead. He commanded us to preach to the people and to testify that he is the one ordained by God as judge of the living and the dead. All the prophets testify about him that everyone who believes in him receives forgiveness of sins through his name. (Acts 10:40–43)

A departing Jesus commissions failing disciples in a farewell discourse delivered at the last of a long series of meals that Jesus has shared with broken people. The message is clear:

> Jesus will not distance himself from them because they fail him. The keynote of his ministry, and especially his table fellowship has been 'He was reckoned with transgressors' (Is 53:12; Lk 22:37), both by his own desire and the will of his persecutors (see 23:32). And he will continue to share his life with sinners in the kingdom meals of the time of the Church.[28]

THE LAST SUPPER IN JOHN

The claim is often made that there is no eucharistic passage in John's account of Jesus's final evening with his disciples, despite the fact that the words and events of that evening occupy five chapters of the Gospel (John 13:1—17:26). Careful scrutiny of 13:1–38—the account of Jesus washing the disciples' feet, the gift of the morsel to Judas, and the words of Jesus (and the disciples) associated with these two events—indicates that a powerful early Christian understanding of baptism and Eucharist lies behind this famous passage.[29]

The key to interpreting this passage is 13:1: "Jesus knew that his hour had come to depart from this world and go to the Father. Having loved his own who were in the world, he loved them to the end." Jesus's loving "to the end" (Greek: *eis telos*) has two meanings, and both are intended. It means that he loved them without hesitation till his very last breath on the cross. But it also means that he loved them in a consummate fashion: "to the end" in the sense that his love for his own is beyond description. A second important guide to a reading of this passage is the use of the expression "Amen, amen, I say to you." Unfortunately, reducing the double "amen" to "very truly," the NRSV hides a unique Johannine literary characteristic. Only John uses "*amen, amen*, I say to you." A similar expression is found with one "amen" in the Synoptic Gospels, especially in Matthew (thirty-one times). In John, the double "amen" appears thirteen times, and four of those appearances are found in 13:1–38 (vv. 16–17, 20, 21, and 38).

The expression marks the beginning or the end of sections in a narrative as it unfolds.[30] The four uses of the double "amen" in 13:1–38 shape its literary structure.[31]

Verses 1–17: Jesus washes the disciples' feet and follows this action with words that close with the first double "amen" statement in verses 16–17.

Verses 18–20: Jesus explains his actions to his fragile disciples, closing with the second double "amen" in verse 20.

Verses 21–38: Jesus gives the morsel to Judas and follows this action with words to his disciples. This passage opens (v. 21) and closes (v. 38) with the third and fourth use of the double "amen."

THE FOOT-WASHING AND ITS AFTERMATH (VERSES 1–17)

A declaration of love heads the account of Jesus's washing the disciples' feet and giving the morsel to Judas. Its first narrative section, ending with the typically Johannine double "amen" (vv. 16–17), unfolds in three parts, featuring shifts in events and major players.

1. *Verses 1–5*: John announces that Jesus "knows" that the hour of his departure to the Father has come. What is about to be told will indicate the consummate perfection of Jesus's love for his own (v. 1). These words are immediately followed by an indication that the devil had already decided in his heart that Judas would betray Jesus (v. 2). Too often the translators report that "the devil had already put it into the heart of Judas." This does not correctly render the Greek,[32] and disturbs the narrative. It is not until verse 27, after Judas takes the morsel, that Satan enters him. "Knowing" these things does not deter Jesus from moving into action. He prepares himself and washes the disciples' feet (vv. 3–5). Jesus's *love* (v. 1) and *knowledge* (vv. 1, 3) flow into *action* (vv. 4–5).
2. *Verses 6–11*: Peter objects to Jesus's washing his feet, and Jesus dialogues with him (vv. 6–10b). Here, the link between the foot-washing and the practice of baptism emerges. Peter can "have no part" with Jesus, unless he is prepared to be washed by Jesus (v. 8). Through the foot-washing, the disciple "has part" in the saving effects of Jesus's death and resurrection.[33] This leads to Jesus's first statement on Judas's future betrayal (vv. 10c–11).
3. *Verses 12–17*: Jesus instructs the disciples on the significance of what he has done for them and asks that they do the same, following his example (vv. 12–15). The pattern of teacher and lord kneeling in self-gift for his own must continue as a mark of the followers of Jesus. He has given them an example they are to repeat in their lives of service,

no matter what their future roles might be. The choice of the Greek word for "example" (*hypodeigma*) in verse 15 continues the theme of self-gift in love, even to death. The Greek expression, found only in John 13:15 in the entire New Testament, appears in some well-known Jewish texts that speak of exemplary death (LXX 1 Macc 6:28; 4 Macc 17:22–23; Sir 44:16). "Jesus' death..., as it is here interpreted through the foot-washing, is the norm of life and conduct for the believing community."[34] The double "amen" closes the section that has asked that disciples be servants of their master, blessed by a knowledge that flows into action (John 13:16–17). As the section opened, Jesus's love and knowledge flowed into action in verses 1–5. In a beautifully balanced sentence, it closes with his words to the disciples: "If you *know* these things, **blessed are you** if you *do* them" (v. 17 RSV).[35] As Jesus has demonstrated love in action in the foot-washing, he has given them an example: they are to demonstrate love in action by following his example—to the end (v. 15; see v. 1).

THE CENTRAL STATEMENT (VERSES 18–20)

The stunning centerpiece of John 13:1–38 is found in verses 18–20. Between verses 1–17 and verses 21–38, the rationale for both the servile washing of the feet of fragile and misunderstanding disciples, especially Simon Peter, and the gift of the morsel to Judas is spelt out. The passage presents three affirmations:

1. *Verse 18*: Jesus has *chosen* fragile disciples, one of whom will betray him.
2. *Verse 19*: Why he has done this: "That...you may believe that I am he."
3. *Verse 20*: Solemnly introducing his words with the double "amen," Jesus *sends out* these disciples, that both Jesus and the one who sent him may be received.

In verses 18 and 20, Jesus speaks of his relationship with the disciples. He knows whom he has chosen, and he is aware that one of them will strike out against him. He recalls Psalm 41:9, stating that one of them, who shares the table and eats (Greek: *ho trōgōn*) his bread, has lifted his heel against him (John 13:18). I indicate the Greek verb (*trōgōn*) because John has consciously altered the verb he found in the Greek Bible (LXX). The original uses the correct word for human eating (*esthiō*), but John has adopted a cruder verb, indicating the physical "munching" with the teeth. The importance of John's alteration will appear on arrival at verses 26–27. The betrayer, who has lurked throughout this narrative (see vv. 2, 10c–11), is again mentioned in verse 18. Despite the failures and the betrayals, however, *Jesus has chosen these disciples.* In verse 20, he points out that he has not only chosen them (v. 18), but he will send them out (v. 20). Closing this central section with a further double "amen," Jesus assures them that he sends them out so that they can make Jesus known, just as Jesus has made the Father known. Anyone who receives his sent ones, therefore, will also receive the Father. *Jesus will send out these disciples to make known both the Father and the Son.* For this remarkable mission, Jesus has chosen and sent out ignorant, fragile disciples, even one who will betray him.

The question "why" must be asked. To choose and send out those who fail, betray, and deny makes no sense. The response to that question is provided in verse 19 (the central statement of 13:1–38): "I tell you this now, before it occurs, so that *when it does occur, you may believe that I am he* (Greek: *hoti egō eimi*)." In Jesus's act of foot-washing, symbolizing his consummate love-unto-death for disciples who fail to understand and who will betray him, the God and Father of Jesus is revealed.[36] It will shortly be matched by the gift of the morsel to Judas. This gesture also tells of self-gift unto death for disciples who do not understand him, who betray him, and deny him (vv. 21–38). As yet, the unconditional self-gift of Jesus on the cross for his fragile disciples has not taken place, but is anticipated in the loving gestures of the washing of the feet and the gift of the morsel. The audience is well aware that what is anticipated by these gestures will take place on the cross, but the disciples are not. They continue in their ignorance, their false promises, and their misunderstanding. But Jesus tells them that he is giving himself to them in the symbols of the washing and the gift of the morsel, so that at a later time, they might come to believe that he makes known the consummate love of God. They remain in their sin "now," but there will be a time "afterwards," when they will be forgiven, and they will believe that Jesus's loving self-gift is a revelation of God.

The post-Easter Johannine community knows that Jesus has chosen disciples, and sent them out as bearers of his presence, and the presence of the Father who sent him (vv. 18, 20). He is telling his disciples in the story all these things *now*, before the event of the cross. *Afterward*, when that consummate revelation of love takes place, they might believe that he is the presence of the divine among them (v. 19: "that I am he"). If the earlier statements about the countercultural nature of Jesus's actions in his example to the disciples are surprising (vv. 12–15), his revelation of why he is giving himself unconditionally in love to disciples, chosen and sent out by him, who not only do not love him in the same way, but who will deny him, betray him, and misunderstand him, transcends all possible human explanation. This is what it means to love *to the end* (v. 1), consummately, in a way that the world can never comprehend. The love of Jesus for his own *to the end* is the revelation of the incomprehensible love of God. In these gestures of loving self-gift, anticipating the cross, Jesus makes known the love of God. They demonstrate Jesus's love in action to a stunned audience *of the story*, who are themselves fragile disciples of Jesus. But verses 18–20 instruct them that they, like the original disciples, are chosen (v. 18), forgiven (v. 19), and sent (v. 20).

THE GIFT OF THE MORSEL AND ITS AFTERMATH (VERSES 21–38)

Matching the structure of verses 1–17, the closing section of John 13:1–38 also has three parts:

1. *Verses 21–25*: The narrator indicates Jesus's profound emotional condition. Opening with a double "amen," Jesus again forecasts the future betrayal of Judas, creating "uncertainty" among all the disciples (vv. 21–22). The Greek word for "uncertain" (*aporoumenoi*) is very strong: "perplexed" or "confused." From his place of intimacy "reclining next to him" (see 1:18), at the request of Simon Peter, the beloved disciple asks who this might be. He too, does not understand what is happening (vv. 23–25).
2. *Verses 26–30*: Jesus indicates that he will give the morsel to his betrayer, and proceeds to do so (v. 26). Matching the dialogue between Jesus and Simon Peter in verses 6–10a, a

brief dialogue between Jesus and Judas follows (vv. 26–30), but it opens with the gift of the morsel (v. 26). The Greek manuscripts, and many translations, have attempted to lessen the impression that this gift of the morsel has a eucharistic significance by dropping the words "he took and." They need to be restored to our translations. Thus, catching up words used in all early Christian reports of the Last Supper, John reports, "So when he dipped the piece of bread, he took and gave it to Judas, son of Simon Iscariot" (v. 26b AT).[37] In verse 18, Jesus cited the Greek version of Psalm 41:9 that spoke about the betrayal of one who "eats" at the table of the one betrayed. However, as indicated above, John's use is not the normal verb for human eating. He shifts to the use of a Greek verb that refers to the physical munching and crunching with the teeth (*trōgō*). The only other place where this appears in the Gospel is 6:51–58, where Jesus teaches explicitly about the Eucharist: "Those who eat [*trōgōn*] my flesh and drink my blood have eternal life, and I will raise them up on the last day; for my flesh is true food and my blood is true drink. Those who eat [*trōgōn*] my flesh and drink my blood abide in me, and I in them" (6:54–56). John wants to make it very clear to his audience that Jesus gives himself unconditionally to the most despised character in the Gospel in a gesture that matches their celebration of Eucharist. Only now does Satan enter into Judas (v. 27). As Jesus responds to God (see v. 1), Judas is now involved in a satanic agenda (see v. 2). John comments that "no one" at the table understood what was happening, despite the obvious sign of the gift of the morsel. There is profound obtuseness on the part of all the disciples, including the beloved disciple (vv. 28–29). After receiving the morsel, Judas goes out into the darkness of the night (v. 30).

3. *Verses 31–38*: As Judas departs, the passion begins. Judas's departure to betray Jesus sets off the process of Jesus's passion that will lead to the cross (v. 31a). As John understands the cross as Jesus's perfection of the task given to him (see 4:34; 19:30), Jesus announces that the moment

> of the glorification of the Son of Man and the revelation of the glory of God is "now" (vv. 31b–32). Addressing these frail disciples with a very affectionate term, "little children" (Greek: *teknia*), he informs them that shortly he will depart from them, and they will search for him in vain (v. 33). He then issues a new commandment that should highlight their way of life in his absence. They are to love one another as he has loved them (vv. 34–35), as after the foot-washing he had instructed them to follow his "example" (v. 15). Peter continues to misunderstand Jesus's destiny, marked by his imminent departure. He insists that wherever Jesus is going, he will follow. Recalling his earlier words to Peter in verse 7, and to all the disciples in verse 19, he indicates that he does not understand "now," but he will "afterwards." Closing this section with a final double "amen," the proximate further failure of Peter is foretold: he will deny Jesus three times before cock-crow (v. 38).

For centuries, Christians read John 13:1–38 as if it were an exact report of what actually took place on that night and were horrified by the suggestion that Jesus might have shared the eucharistic morsel with Judas. Given the variety of eucharistic traditions that we have, and the central liturgical significance of the "memorial" of this meal across the Christian centuries, it is impossible to establish from the data of the New Testament *what actually took place* at the meal that night. As in the early Church and subsequent centuries, many contemporary Christians continue to be shocked by an interpretation that suggests a eucharistic background to Jesus's gift of the morsel to Judas in John 13:26. We must recognize that John has given a significant account of the overwhelming enormity of God's love, manifested in and through Jesus. In his usual insightful fashion, St. Augustine provided the Christian Tradition with this interpretation: "Why was the bread given to the traitor, but as a demonstration of the grace he had treated with ingratitude?"[38]

A blow-by-blow reconstruction of what Jesus may or may not have done on that night cannot be determined, nor is it helpful as we search for the message communicated to us by the inspired Word of God found in Paul and the Gospels.[39] Largely unrecognized, however, is the fact that in the Synoptic Gospels, Judas has already associated himself with the plot to kill Jesus (Mark 14:10–11; Matt 26:14–16; Luke 22:3–6), but he is present at the last meal (Mark 14:17–21; Matt 26:20–25; Luke 22:14, 21–23). Indeed, Luke has Jesus state, "The one who betrays me is with me, and his hand is on the table" (Luke 22:21).

THE RISEN LORD AND THE EUCHARIST AS A CELEBRATION OF FORGIVENESS

A feature of Luke's resurrection account is his insistence that everything took place *on the one day* (see Luke 24:1, 13, 29, 36, 51). The whole of Luke's Gospel has been directed toward this "day." As Jesus began his journey toward Jerusalem in Luke 9:51, the narrator commented, "When the days drew near for him to be received up, he set his face to go to Jerusalem" (RSV). On this resurrection "day," we sense that we are at the end of a long journey. The Lukan use of this theme is at the center of his account of the journey of two disciples to Emmaus (24:13–35).[40]

The opening remarks of the journey to Emmaus are an indication of the wrong choice made by two disciples. "That very day"—in the midst of the paschal events—two disciples were going to Emmaus, "about seven miles [sixty stadia] from Jerusalem" (24:13 RSV). They are walking *away from Jerusalem*, the central point of God's story, away from God's journey, making himself known in his Son from Nazareth (Luke 1—2) to the ends of the earth (Acts 1:8; 28:16–31). The paschal events are in the forefront of the disciples' minds, and the subject of their conversation, as they walk (v. 14), and as the risen Jesus joins them, and "went with them" (v. 15). As the risen one, he "walks with" two disciples who are abandoning God's saving story. God is behind this encounter. Luke does not say that they were unable to recognize Jesus, but that "their eyes were kept from recognizing him" (v. 16). There is a mysterious "other" directing the presence of Jesus with disciples, indicated by the use of the divine passive voice of the verb. Jesus opens the conversation by asking them what they were discussing with one another as they walked. At Jesus's question, they stop (v. 16).

A hint of something new has entered the story, but it does not last, as one of them, named Cleopas, responds to Jesus's question. He wonders how Jesus could even ask such a question. Surely, every visitor to Jerusalem would know "the things that have taken place there in these days" (v. 18). There is incredible irony as Cleopas asks Jesus, who had journeyed from Galilee to the city and was indeed a visitor to Jerusalem, to bring to a climax part of God's saving design. This journey has been under way since 9:51, when Jesus set his face for Jerusalem, "[as] the days drew near for him to be received up" (RSV). He asks the very "visitor," to whom these events happened, why he does not know about them. Jesus, who has been at the center of the events, is also the measure of their significance. But the two disciples know only of the "events," not what God has done through them. Indeed, "their eyes were kept from recognizing him" (24:16).

A catechetical-liturgical process begins in verse 19 where, in response to Jesus's further query about the events, they show their extent of their knowledge of "what has happened" in Jerusalem. Crucial to their response to Jesus is their explanation of their expectations of Jesus: "We had hoped that he was the one to redeem Israel" (v. 21). They have not understood the significance of the life, teaching, death, and resurrection of Jesus. His way of responding to the Father has not fulfilled their hopes for the one who would redeem Israel. But they do know of *the facts* of his life, teaching, death, and resurrection.

- They know of his life, teaching, and miraculous ministry: Jesus of Nazareth, a prophet mighty in word and deed (v. 19).
- They know of his death: "Our chief priests and rulers delivered him up to be condemned to death, and crucified him" (v. 20 RSV).
- They know of the events at the tomb: "It is now the third day" (v. 21). Women have been at the tomb early in the morning, but "they...did not find his body" (v. 23).
- They have even heard the Easter proclamation: there has been a vision of angels who said, "He [is] alive!" (v. 23).
- If, perhaps, the witness of the women was not enough, "some of those who were with us" have been to the tomb and found it empty. "But him they did not see" (v. 24).

The two disciples on the way to Emmaus know everything, but they did not see him (vv. 15–17). Thus, they do not understand the *significance* of these *events*, and they continue their walk away from Jerusalem.

Jesus chides them for their foolishness. He opens the Scriptures for them, explaining that it was necessary that the Christ should suffer many things to enter his glory (vv. 25–26). He "interpreted to them the things about himself in all the scriptures" (v. 27). Jesus journeys with these disciples who have abandoned God's journey, and on the way, a "liturgy of the Word" takes place. He calls to their memory the necessity for the Christ to suffer in order to enter into his glory (v. 26). Not only did Jesus teach these truths (see 9:22, 44; 18:31–33), but it was the true meaning of "all the Scriptures," beginning with Moses and the prophets (24:27).

The narrative has reached a turning point. Initiative must come from the erring disciples themselves. Has the word of Jesus made any impact on them? The Greek of verse 28 reads, "He pretended to be going further." Jesus has opened the Word of God for them. The disciples must now take some initiative in response to Jesus's explanation of the Word. They do so generously: "Stay with us, because it is almost evening and the day is now nearly over" (v. 29). As the evening of the Easter "day" draws in, the littleness of faith that led them to leave Jerusalem and the eleven is being overcome by the presence of the risen Lord (v. 15) and his opening of the Word (vv. 25–27). A process of repentance and forgiveness is underway, generated by the action of Jesus who walks with his fragile disciples.

At the meal, the disciples recognize him in the breaking of the bread (vv. 30–31). The memory of the many meals that Jesus has shared with them, and especially the meal he shared on the night before he died (22:14–38), opens their eyes and anticipates the many meals that will be celebrated in the future. Touched by Jesus's word and presence in their failure, the failing disciples turn back on their journey: "That same hour they got up and returned to Jerusalem" (v. 33). The journey "away from Jerusalem" (v. 13) has been reversed as they turn back "to Jerusalem" (v. 33). Once they arrive at the place they should never have abandoned and are with the eleven apostles upon whom the community is founded, before they can even utter a word about their experience, they find that Easter faith is already alive. They are told, "The Lord has risen indeed, and he has appeared to Simon" (v. 34). Easter faith has already been born in Jerusalem.

As the Gospel opens, the reader/listener comes to know of a man called "Simon" (4:38). Within the context of a miraculous catch of fish, he is called to be a disciple of Jesus and Jesus introduces a new name for him "Peter" (see 5:8). The audience is reminded of this transformation in the Lukan list of the twelve apostles: "Simon, whom he named Peter" (6:14). From that point on, throughout the whole of the Gospel, he is called "Peter" (see 8:45, 51; 9:20, 28, 32–33; 12:41; 18:28). At the Last Supper, where the mingling of the themes of Jesus's sharing his table with the broken and the commissioning of his future apostles is found, he is still "Peter" (22:8, 34, 54, 55, 58, 60–61). Only in foretelling his future denials does Jesus emphatically revert to the name he had before he became a disciple: "Simon, Simon, listen! Satan has demanded to sift all of you like wheat" (22:31). It is to the failed "Simon" that the risen Lord has appeared, to restore him to his apostolic role (24:34). The name "Simon," without any link to the apostolic name "Peter," appears only before this man's call to be a follower of Jesus (4:18) and at the end of the Emmaus story, when two failing disciples are restored to God's saving story that takes place in Jerusalem (24:34). The failed disciples have returned to another disciple who had failed his Lord. This return home, however, has happened because the risen Lord reached out to them in their brokenness and made himself known to them in the breaking of the bread.

It is to these sinful, yet forgiven disciples that the risen Jesus appears, instructs them on the true meaning of the Scriptures, and shares a meal with them (vv. 36–46).[41] As Jesus prepares to leave them in his return to his Father, he commissions them to proclaim repentance and the forgiveness of sins to all nations (v. 47). They are eminently qualified to proclaim the celebration of forgiveness, as they have been the first to enjoy that celebration. Jesus can thus both inform them and instruct them: "You are witnesses of these things" (v. 48). They have witnessed forgiveness in their own eucharistic encounter with Jesus (vv. 13–35, 36–46). As such, they can be the best of all witnesses of this forgiveness to all the nations.

CONCLUSION

The earliest witness to a "Theology of the Eucharist" comes to us from Paul's First Letter to the Corinthians (c. 54 CE). The Gospel narratives of Mark (c. 70 CE), Matthew (late 80s CE), Luke (late 80s CE), and John (c. 100 CE) continue to develop the early Church's reflection on the significance of Jesus's ongoing and loving self-gift made available in what was quickly called "Eucharist," a word associated with thanksgiving. It was celebrated in many places and many ways as the Church developed. Already in the New Testament, we have evidence of at least three liturgical traditions (Matthew/Mark, Paul/Luke, and John). Too much is sometimes made of the actual "words of institution" in the Gospels. The participation at the shared meal, with *all that was associated with the meal*, is what matters. It was some centuries before the so-called words of institution became an integral part of the celebration.

The theme of Jesus's forgiving presence to his failing disciples in Mark and Matthew, Luke's use of the same theme to appoint these sinful apostles as his missionaries, and the Johannine Jesus's presence to disciples who betray, deny, and do not understand him reach beyond the "words of institution." They form the essential context for the meal and embody the central message of the Gospels' portrait of Jesus forgiving presence to his sinful followers on the night before he died.

CHAPTER 3

Proclaiming Repentance and Forgiveness

So far, we have looked at the message of the New Testament, with its roots in the life and practice of Jesus of Nazareth, that the Table of the Lord was a place where the unity of the Christian community was celebrated, generated by the loving self-gift of Jesus (1 Cor 10:1—11:34; Mark 6:31–44; 8:1–10; Matt 14:13–21; 15:32–39). We have consequently seen that Jesus's final evening with his disciples introduced the darkest night in the history of Christianity: Jesus's chosen disciples betrayed him, denied him, and deserted him (Mark 14:17–21, 26–31; Matt 26:20–25, 30–35; Luke 22:14, 21–23, 31–34). He nevertheless celebrated a Last Supper with them, instructed them that in the broken body and spilled blood that would become a reality on the following day, he was setting up a new covenant with them (Mark 14:22–25; Matt 26:26–29; Luke 22:20). Their sins would be forgiven (Matt 26:28) and they would be sent out by Jesus (John 13:20), bearers of a message of repentance and forgiveness to all the nations (Luke 24:36–46).

But this is not the *only* impression left by the New Testament witnesses. We have seen that Paul is concerned about the "worthiness" of the Corinthians' celebration of the Eucharist. In their case, the problem arose from their neglecting the poorer members of the community (1 Cor 11:17–22). There are two further New Testament texts that indicate the practice of excluding certain people from the community: Paul's words on the expulsion of the man involved in an incestuous relationship from the Corinthian community (1 Cor 5:1–8) and the warning against apostasy from the author of the Letter to the Hebrews

(Heb 8:1–13).[1] Such exclusion refused access to the Lord's Table, even if this is not stated.[2]

There was, from the beginning of the Christian movement, a sense of the sacredness of a celebration that recalled the saving effects of the death and resurrection of Jesus.[3] The Lord's Table was the crucial symbol of the oneness of the body of a community that shared in the one bread and the one cup, a place where divisions were to be put aside, and where the fragile were forgiven and nourished for their Christian journey and mission. But from the beginning, it was also a sacred ritual and experience. A desire to safeguard the holiness of the Lord's Supper is found in the apostolic fathers (early to mid-second century), the apologists (second and third centuries), into the era of the fathers of the Church. A study of Eucharist as the celebration of forgiveness must also recognize the Christian Tradition of safeguarding the holiness of the Lord's Table by calling for repentance.

EXCLUSION FROM THE COMMUNITY IN THE NEW TESTAMENT

1 CORINTHIANS 5:1–8

Paul uses his First Letter to the Corinthians to discuss a number of issues that he regarded as central to their new lives as Christians. He systematically introduces issues by referring to reports that he has had from Corinth, or explicitly raising questions that concern him in their regard (see 1:10–11; 5:1a; 7:1; 8:1; 11:18; 12:1; 15:1). He opens his discussion of sexual behavior, marriage, and divorce (5:1—7:40) with reference to a report he has received concerning totally unacceptable sexual behavior: "A man is living with his father's wife" (5:1c). Paul rhetorically continues, "If this is the case, then you are worse than the pagans!" (v. 1b AT). "The pagans serve only as a foil for the sharpness of his judgment concerning the case in the community."[4] Incest had no place in a community that based its ethical practice on the biblical traditions of Israel (see Lev 18:8; 20:11). Paul is dependent on Leviticus 18. The prohibitions of LXX Leviticus 18:8 and 20:11 refer to the wife of the father and LXX Leviticus 18:24 legislates expulsion.

Paul's interaction with the Corinthians to this point in his letter enables him to accuse them of arrogance (v. 2), repeating his accusation of 4:18: "Some of you, thinking I am not coming to you, have become arrogant." The themes of arrogance and a sense of false superiority have been strongly present in the letter to this point (see 1:12, 18–31; 3:3–9, 18–21; 4:6, 18). The Corinthian Christians, in their newfound freedom, regard matters of the flesh as of no significance (see 6:12; 10:23).[5] In the face of such possible sin, this is a false response. It should lead to expulsion from the community. Paul is psychologically present, even in absence. As such, he has already made a judgment on what should happen in such a case (5:3) "in the name of the Lord Jesus" (v. 4a). Paul's reaction to the possibility that a serious moral sin has been allowed to continue in the Christian community is driven by more than ethical opinion; it comes from an authority based in the life and teaching of Jesus Christ.[6]

Paul continues a theologically motivated argument. He indicates that his judgment must be made by the assembly of the community that gathers "with the power of our Lord Jesus" (v. 4), and with Paul present "in spirit" (v. 3). The existence and authority of the community come from "the Lord Jesus." The risen Lord authorizes the community to "hand this man over to Satan" (v. 5a). Although a Jewish practice, expulsion in the Corinthian community must be *christologically motivated.*[7] The community only exists because of the "preliminary defeat of Satan by Jesus (15:24–27; Phil 2:10–11; Col 2, 15)."[8] As a result of the free gift of God that took place in the death and resurrection of Jesus (see Rom 3:21–26), there are two possible "spheres of existence." One can live in the freedom and grace generated by the obedience manifested in Jesus's death and resurrection, or in the world of sin and slavery to sin generated by the disobedience and sin of Adam (see Rom 5:12–21). Once in the latter world, the world of Satan, the man heads inexorably to the final destruction of his flesh: death (v. 5b).

Such a man, however, is to be dismissed for a reason: "that his spirit may be saved in the day of the Lord" (v. 5c). The man's physical death may not bring about his salvation "in the day of the Lord," but the death and resurrection of Jesus might. Paul is anxious about the purity of the community (see vv. 6–7), but the final salvation of the sinful man is also a major concern. As Kingsley Barrett puts it:

> For Paul atonement is not through our death, but through Christ's. The thought may be that the devil must be given his due, but can claim no more; if he has the flesh he has no right

> to the spirit, even of the sinner....the man's essential self will be saved with the loss not only of his work but of his flesh.[9]

The action of the Spirit-filled community, authorized by the risen Lord (v. 4b), is to initiate a process that leads to life, despite the man's current situation, given "over to Satan" (v. 5a).

Beginning his instructions with an example taken from everyday domestic experience (v. 6), Paul moves to the profound theological and christological reason for the elimination of the sinner (vv. 7–8). He informs the arrogant Corinthians that all one needs to generate a full loaf of bread is a small amount of yeast in the dough. It permeates the whole loaf (v. 6; see also Gal 5:9).[10] Paul's concern is the well-being and sound Christian life and practice of the community. At the Jewish Passover, all yeast was removed from the household before the celebration (see Exod 12:8, 15, 17–20, 34, 39; 13:3, 6–7; 23:15; 34:18). Paul uses this practice to instruct the community, so that its members may remain pure, a "new batch" of unleavened dough, uncontaminated because all leaven that could permeate the community has been eliminated. But mention of the Passover allows Paul to turn to the issue that dominates all his thought and instruction: the death and resurrection of Jesus Christ (see Phil 3:7–11).

He makes a theological link between the "new batch" of unleavened dough and Jesus's obedient sacrifice unto death: "Our paschal lamb, Christ, has been sacrificed" (v. 7). The Christian community, freed from sin by the saving action of Christ, must behave in a way that demonstrates their freedom from sin. Jesus, the paschal sacrifice, has set them free: "For freedom Christ has set us free. Stand firm, therefore, and do not submit again to a yoke of slavery" (Gal 5:1). The sacrifice of the paschal lamb gives authority and freedom, but the consequent moral response of the community must take place; otherwise, the christological truth makes no impact on Christian life. "The indicative is emasculated if the imperative, which gives it moral bite, is wanting."[11]

Closing his argument, Paul tells the Corinthians to celebrate the Passover joyfully, aware of what they are celebrating. The Passover celebrated in the Corinthian community is one that recalls the death and resurrection of Jesus.[12] By all means celebrate, Paul says (v. 8a), but recognize that this is a "new Passover" in which those who have been freed from sin by the death and resurrection of Jesus have eliminated "the yeast of malice and evil." They are now "the unleavened bread of sincerity and truth," no longer rendered impure by the presence of a sinner in their midst (v. 8b).

"The presence within the community of an attitude incompatible with Christ puts the freedom of all at risk because the protective barrier against the value system of the 'world' (= 'Sin') has been weakened."[13] Such a flagrant moral disorder cannot be tolerated *for christological reasons*. A community that is based on the self-sacrificing love of Jesus—the paschal lamb (see 11:23–25)—must live in constant recognition of that fact.[14]

> The community has gone over from the sphere of death and flesh, the old context, to the new context of life and the spirit. The consequence ought to be: He who does not want to walk in the new context has by this himself chosen to stay in the old.[15]

HEBREWS 6:1–8

The Letter to the Hebrews argues for the superiority of Christ over every other power.[16] The centerpiece of the letter is found in Hebrews 5:11—10:39, although the argument pursued across these verses is not reserved to that passage. Hebrews 5:11—10:39 focuses strongly on the perfection of what God has done for Israel in the "once and for all" sacrifice of Jesus. More urgently than anywhere else in Hebrews, the author argues for the saving effects of the sacrifice of Jesus Christ and his ultimate Lordship.[17] After the memorable presentation of Jesus as the unique High Priest (4:14—5:10) that closes the previous literary unit (3:1—5:10), a new section of the homily begins with an exhortation to overcome a "dullness of understanding" (see 5:11), to develop a new maturity, "trained by practice to distinguish good from evil" (5:14).

Framed by positive exhortations that describe the difference between infants and the mature who are ready to go beyond the fundamentals of Christian life and belief (5:11—6:3), and the confidence in a just God that should enable greater maturity, who "will not overlook your work and the love that you showed for his sake in serving the saints, as you still do" (6:10; see vv. 9–12), in verses 4–8, the author addresses the dire consequences of falling away:

> For it is impossible to restore again to repentance those who have once been enlightened and have taken the heavenly gift,

> and have shared in the Holy Spirit, and have tasted the goodness of the word of God and the powers of the age to come, and then have fallen away, since on their own they are crucifying the Son of God and are holding him up to contempt. Ground that drinks up the rain falling on it repeatedly, and that promotes a crop useful to those for whom it is cultivated receives a blessing from God. But if it produces thorns and thistles, it is worthless and on the verge of being cursed; its end is to be burned over. (Heb 6:4–8, AT)

Hebrews 6:4–8 is not a condemnation of a specific person or group of persons. Rather, it is a dramatic presentation of the *possibility* that some who have experienced the fullness of Christian life (vv. 4–5) *might* fall away (v. 6). It would be impossible (Greek: *adunaton*) to restore them to the community, through an act of repentance (v. 4). Like useless ground that produces no crop, in the end, they will be "burned over" (vv. 7–8).

For whom is it impossible to restore such a fallen Christian? For the apostate by means of repentance? For the Christian community? For God? The passage must be understood as indicating that God "for whom and through whom all things exist" (2:10), whose word can shake heaven and earth (see 12:26), *could* do whatever God wants, but will not. God refuses to restore the apostate, one who has tasted the treasures of grace, life in the Holy Spirit, the Word of God, and the promises of the life to come (vv. 4–5).[18]

Over the centuries, in heated debates over those whose faith "lapsed" in time of persecution, or as Christianity divided in the sixteenth century, Hebrews 6:4–8 has been used and abused. The text must be located within its literary context. Immediately prior to the passage on apostasy (vv. 1–3), the author exhorts the audience to greater maturity in their Christian lives. They are to grow beyond the basics that they have received and practiced (vv. 1–2).[19] The immediate following context (vv. 9–12) opens with these words: "Even though we speak in this way, beloved, we are confident of better things in your case, things that belong to salvation" (v. 9). In verses 4–8, the author is not addressing apostates, but believing and "beloved" Christians. The harsh words of verses 4–8 do not address a concrete situation. As Craig Koester states,

> The warning about apostasy and the promise of God's faithfulness function differently—the warning disturbs while the promise gives assurance—but they serve the same end, which is that listeners might persevere in faith (6:12).[20]

The author is not saying that this situation pertained among his audience. However, what he describes should be regarded as the way unforgivable apostasy could take place. The author does not "invent" what he describes to his beloved audience (v. 8), warning them against all possible danger (vv. 4–8). It is possible what he describes were the actions performed by apostates, perhaps within the context of persecution, even though they have been generalized for the present context.[21] In our search to uncover the early Church's care for the holiness of the community, and thus of its eucharistic celebrations, this text retains its importance, however "hypothetical" the warning might be.

Hebrews 6:1–13 is concerned with "perfection, leaving behind the basic teaching about Christ" (v. 1). In their journey to mature Christianity (vv. 1–3), and the faith and patience that are signs of that maturity (vv. 9–13), they may encounter the risk of apostasy (vv. 4–8). The apostates "crucify the Son of God on their own account and hold him up to contempt" (v. 6 AT).[22] It is possible that Christians who have enjoyed all the privileges of the Christian life (vv. 4–5), can continue the arrogance and unbelief of the crucifiers of Jesus. It is impossible to restore such apostates to repentance (v. 6). They are like a well-watered field that has received God's gifts, but has produced only thorns. They will be destroyed (vv. 6–8) because they reject Jesus Christ. As Brooke F. Westcott has suggested, "Perhaps there is the further thought in the image of crucifixion that Christ dwells in the believer. To fall away from faith is therefore to slay him."[23]

The earliest Church encountered division and apostasy, and dealt with it as best it could.[24] The criterion for exclusion was the rejection of the fundamental beliefs that shaped Christianity: Jesus is the Christ, the Son of God, and Savior (see, e.g., Rom 1:1–4; Mark 1:1; Matt 16:16; Luke 9:20; John 4:42; 20:30–31). Both 1 Corinthians 5:1–8 and Hebrews 6:4–8 indicate that deliberate sinfulness, and the necessary subsequent exclusion, would be caused by a faulty Christology. For Paul, this faulty Christology also led to an "arrogant" community, and thus a faulty Ecclesiology (see 1 Cor 5:2, 6). The holiness of the community, brought into existence through the death and resurrection of Jesus, was recognized and defended against those who would not accept what God had done in and through Jesus.

The measure of "worthiness" for membership in the Christian community was faith in what God had done in and through Jesus Christ. From the first disciples onward, God's gracious gift of Jesus Christ and the forgiveness associated with it (see Matt 26:28) have been misunderstood (John 13:1–38), abused (1 Cor 5:1–8), and rejected (Heb 6:4–8). God's promise of forgiveness is not withdrawn, but it calls for repentance (Luke 24:36–46).

THE TRADITION CONTINUES

A detailed analysis of the criteria for exclusion from the community and/or its table adopted by the apostolic fathers and the so-called apologists of the second century, the earlier fathers of the third century, and the great masters of the fourth and fifth centuries, lies outside the scope of this study. The material is voluminous, and there were significant differences in opinion, cultures, and practice across these formative centuries. The following reflection focusses on the earlier period, and then selects representative samples from the later centuries.[25] This sketch suggests that, among many rich theological and pastoral developments, the Eucharist was an element in the continuing celebration of repentance and forgiveness.

THE *DIDACHE*

The very early Christian document, known today as the *Didache*, is most likely the earliest postbiblical document we have that makes reference to the practice of celebrating a eucharistic meal. Most would accept that it appeared some time about 100 CE, or shortly thereafter.[26] The author instructs his audience on the Eucharist in *Didache* 9:1—10:7. Showing the rapid development of both terminology and practice, he opens his instructions: "Now concerning the Eucharist [Greek: *peri de tēs eucharistias*], give thanks as follows [Greek: *houtō eucharistēsate*]" (9:1). He first instructs on the prayer to be recited over the cup (9:2) and then over the broken bread (9:3–4). In 10:1–6, he provides a prayer of thanksgiving that should be used after people have eaten and drunk sufficiently, allowing the prophets, however, to pray in any form they wish (10:7).[27] Between the prayers over the cup and bread and the closing prayer of benediction, the author inserts the following explicit prohibition:

> For let no one eat or drink of your Eucharist except those who have been baptized into the name of the Lord, for the Lord has also spoken concerning this: "Do not give what is holy to the dogs." (9:5)

The prohibition of sharing the eucharistic meal with the unbaptized is supported by a quotation from the Jesus tradition. It repeats verbatim the text of Matthew 7:6, although some think that it may have come into the tradition that resulted in the *Didache* from oral sources or an unknown Gospel.[28] There is also speculation about who "the dogs" might be, but that need not concern us. A tradition of excluding people from the eucharistic table is in place.[29] The criterion used by the author of the *Didache*, no doubt reflecting the practice of the ecclesial community of the document's origins, is the membership of a Christian community generated by baptism. Participation in the shared cup and the broken bread requires the prior participation in Christian life made possible by insertion into the saving effects of the death and resurrection of Jesus Christ. As with Paul and the author of the Letter to the Hebrews, to be admitted to the Lord's Table one had to *believe* in what God had done in and through the death and resurrection of Jesus.

IGNATIUS OF ANTIOCH

In the first decade of the second century, seven remarkable letters of Ignatius (latter half of the first century—c. 108 CE), bishop of Antioch in Syria, were written across a brief space of time, as he was taken to Rome for execution.[30] They are addressed to Christian communities in Ephesus, Magnesia, Trallia, Rome, Philadelphia, Smyrna, and to Polycarp, bishop in Smyrna. The *Didache* insists on the unity generated by that community celebration: "Just as this broken bread was scattered upon the mountains and then was gathered together and became one, so may your church be gathered together from the ends of the earth into your kingdom" (*Didache* 9:4). The same theme continues in Ignatius, but the figure of the bishop (Greek: *episkopos*), so important to Ignatius, is added to all references to the Eucharist, singled out as a figure that unifies:[31]

> Take care, therefore, to participate in one Eucharist (for there is one flesh of our Lord Jesus Christ, and one cup that leads to unity through his blood; there is one altar, just as there is one bishop, together with the council of presbyters and the deacons, my fellow servants), in order that whatever you do, you do in accordance with God. (*Philadelphians* 4; see also *Ephesians* 5:2; 13:1; 20:2; *Smyrneans* 7:1; 8:1)

According to Ignatius, "Only that Eucharist which is under the authority of the bishop (or whomever he himself designates) is to be considered valid" (*Smyrneans* 8:1).[32]

The Eucharist is not only the center of worship, and the symbol of the unity of the Church, but also "the antidote we take in order not to die but to live forever in Christ" (*Ephesians* 20:2). This is the case because, continuing the Tradition, the bread that is broken reflects the saving effects of the incarnation and the passion (*Trallians* 8:1; *Romans* 7:3; *Philadelphians* 5:1). A consequence of what takes place at the Eucharist is a commitment to good deeds: gentleness, strength in faith, and love (*Smyrneans* 12:2; *Trallians* 8:1).

In his reflections on the role and significance of the celebration of the Eucharist, Ignatius also continues the important tradition of safeguarding the holiness of this gift.[33] He describes his forthcoming martyrdom in terms of the incarnation and the resurrection: "Only let it be in the name of Jesus Christ, so that I may suffer together with him! I endure everything because he himself, who is the perfect human being, empowers me" (*Smyrneans* 4:2). He then writes of "certain people who deny him" (*Smyrneans* 5:1a), raising issues that exclude people from the Christian faith: they are not swayed by the Word of God or the sufferings of the believers (5:1b), they deny the incarnation (5:2), and they do not understand that resurrection of the suffering believer, a fruit of the passion of Jesus (5:3). Such people, possibly docetic seekers of ecclesiastical prestige, do not participate in the "blood" and the "flesh" of Jesus Christ:

> Let no one be misled. Even the heavenly beings and the glory of angels and the rulers, both visible and invisible, are subject

> to judgment if they do not believe in the blood of Christ. Let the one who can accept this accept it. Do not let a high position make anyone proud, for faith and love are everything, nothing is preferable to them.
>
> Now note well those who hold heretical opinions about the grace of Jesus Christ that came to us; note how contrary they are to the mind of God. They have no concern for love, none for the widow, none for the orphan, none for the oppressed, none for the prisoner or the one released, none for the hungry or thirsty. They abstain from Eucharist and prayer because they refuse to acknowledge that the Eucharist is the flesh of our savior Jesus Christ, which suffered for our sins and which the Father by his goodness raised up. (6:1–2)

Ignatius did not need to insist that such people be excluded from the eucharistic meal. They excluded themselves because of their *false doctrines*.[34] An important consequence of this false understanding of the Word of God, the suffering of the believers, and the incarnation (see 5:1–2) was that they paid no attention to the works of love for the poor and abandoned a hallmark of earliest Christianity. Ignatius insists "that the theology of the docetists logically leads to the destruction of what he can take for granted as the aim of all (because it corresponds to the deepest social needs of the early Christians): unity and love."[35] Absence from the Table of the Lord results from a false understanding of *what* God has done for humankind in and through Jesus Christ, and *how* he has done it. A call to repentance and the correction of these views is implicit.

JUSTIN MARTYR

Despite the ongoing possibility of persecution and martyrdom, a number of Christian authors later in the second century began to face the task of interpreting Christianity within the Greco-Roman world. The Christian authors who pursued this task were eventually called the apologists. Important apologists writing in Greek were Justin Martyr (100–165), Tatian (120–80), Athenagoras (133–90), and Clement of Alexandria (150–215).

Justin's *First Apology*, was written between 151–55 CE to the Emperor Antoninus Pius (137–61 CE), appealing against the false charges made against Christians and subsequent unjust violent punishments (*First Apology* 1–12). In his explanation of the nobility of the origins of Christianity, of what Christians believe and do, he closes with a description of their celebrations, to show that their truths and practices that come from Jesus Christ, are not a threat, or strange in any way (65–67).[36] He is the first to indicate what we might nowadays call an "order of service" for the Eucharist, but it can only be taken as an example of what was happening—at least in one place—in Rome at the time. Many such "orders" were being followed in other places, but what is described can be recognized across the developing history of the celebration of the Eucharist.

Justin describes two liturgies. The first takes place after baptism: "after thus washing the one who has been convinced and who has assented to our instruction" (65–66). It is directed by the "Ruler of the Brethren," with all the assembly present. Prayers for the newly baptized are followed by the kiss of peace, and bread, water, and wine mixed with water are taken to the celebrant. Prayers of praise to the Father of the universe, through the Son and the Holy Spirit, and a lengthy thanksgiving are concluded by a solemn "Amen." The bread and wine and water are distributed to those present, and later to those not able to be there. "This food is called among us eucharist" (65–66). The second takes place on a Sunday, and involves all from the city or the countryside who can gather in one place (67). Readings from the apostles and the prophets are followed by instruction and prayers. The rite with bread, water, and wine mixed with water again takes place, followed by the prayers of thanksgiving. Distribution of "the eucharistized elements" are distributed to those present and carried to those absent.[37] The Sunday celebration concludes with a strong link between the Eucharist and the needs of the underprivileged, because "he is the guardian of all those in need." The importance of the link between Sunday and Easter is stressed.

For the purposes of this reflection, baptism remains the criterion for admission to the Eucharist. Participation in the Table of the Lord indicates participation in the saving effects of the crucified and risen Jesus Christ. Only the baptized are worthy of such a privilege. Across these earliest written witnesses to the celebration of the Eucharist, the theme of *faith* in the crucified and risen Lord is the only permanent requirement for "worthiness." This faith is demonstrated by baptism "after assenting to the instruction" (see *First Apology* 65).[38] Such "assent" implies repentance and conversion.

TERTULLIAN

Tertullian (c. 155–c. 240) was an important founding figure of the Latin Christian Tradition. He insisted on the moral worthiness of both the ministers and the participants in the eucharistic celebration.[39] By nature a fiery and demanding figure, he eventually moved away from mainstream Christianity into Montanism, a rigorous sect that accepted new revelations that came from charismatic prophetic figures. The sect held to all the basic beliefs of emerging Christianity, but it demanded the highest of moral standards.[40] In his vigorous and polemical defense of Christian thought, life, and practice in a fashion similar to Justin Martyr, in the thirty-ninth chapter of his *First Apology*, he presents the positive and healthy practices of Christian assemblies, over against the mischief of parallel assemblies of others (the people of Megara, the Salii, the Apaturia, the Dionysiacs, and the Attic mysteries). We cannot be sure that these assemblies are eucharistic, although that is a strong possibility.[41]

He deals with the quality of life expected from those who participate in these assemblies. Tertullian insists on the peace and goodness reflected in the prayers and the gatherings of Christians. They "pray, too, for the emperors, for their ministers and for all in authority, for the welfare of the world, for the prevalence of peace, for the delay of the final consummation."[42] The gatherings are described as places for the improvement of all who are present. The search for a quality Christian life is essential to participation in the gathering:

> For with a great gravity is the work of judging carried on among us, as befits those who feel assured that they are in the sight of God; and you have the most notable example of judgment to come when any one who has sinned so grievously as to require his severance from us in prayer, in the congregation and in all sacred intercourse. (*Apology* 39)

Tertullian is not specific in what he regards as the extent of the grievous sin that causes exclusion. Exclusion comes from Tertullian's conviction that the participants must be "in the sight of God," and living in expectation of the return of the Lord as judge. The exclusion was in itself a means to "educate" believers to overcome sinfulness in order to have a good judgment.[43] In the same document, he insists that the gatherings are directed to the good of the people who participate, and to the needy in society itself. He attacks others who are only interested in their own licentiousness and filling their own bellies. Repeating the widespread early witness of Christian care for the destitute, he claims that the Christians gather "as it is with God himself, a peculiar respect is shown to the lowly." At the conclusion of the celebration of the Eucharist,

> We go from it, not like troops of mischief-doers, nor bands of vagabonds, nor to break out into licentious acts, but to have as much care of our modesty and chastity as if we had been at a school of virtue rather than a banquet. (*Apology* 39)

In his *Prescription against Heretics*, Tertullian rails against those early Christian groups whose assemblies have no sense of order and that are open to anyone: "Today one man is their bishop, tomorrow another, today he is a deacon who tomorrow is a reader; today he is a presbyter who tomorrow is a layman. For even on laymen do they impose the functions of priesthood" (*Prescription* 41).[44] Earlier in this attack, he makes use of Matthew 7:6, in a fashion that matches the use of the same passage (whatever its source) in *Didache* 9:5. With specific reference to "access" to community gatherings to "hear" and to "pray" he writes,

> To begin with, it is doubtful who is a catechumen, and who a believer; they all have access alike, they all hear alike, they pray alike—even heathens, if any such happen to come among them. "That which is holy will be cast to the dogs, and their pearls," although (to be sure) they are not real ones "they will fling to the swine." (*Prescription* 41)

The recognition of the holiness of the community assemblies to pray, to hear, and no doubt to celebrate Eucharist, is a constant theme in the third century.

Equally influential was Tertullian's condemnation of personal sin.[45] It was an offense against the Church that he regarded as the "bride of

Christ," having "neither spot nor wrinkle." Behind his passion is a conviction that essential for admission to Christian celebrations was baptism, adhesion to the community, and to Christian faith and practice. But even for Tertullian, human sinfulness endured after baptism. As he closes his work *On Baptism*, he writes,

> Therefore, blessed ones, when you ascend from that most sacred font of your new birth, and spread your hands for the first time in the house of your mother, together with your brethren, ask from the Father, ask from the Lord, that his own specialties of grace and distributions of gifts may be supplied you. "Ask," says He, "and you shall receive." Well, you have asked, and have received; you have knocked and it has been opened to you. Only, I pray that, when you are asking, you be mindful likewise of Tertullian the sinner. (*On Baptism* 20)[46]

Baptism is a call to sound faith and salvation, but sin is always possible, even though to be avoided and feared. A tradition of repentance and conversion is thus implied by Tertullian's harsh judgment of those who are critical of Christianity, Christians who betray the holiness of the Church, just as he is full of praise of the virtue of the faithful Christians. A tension that can only be resolved by God exists among nonbelievers, sinners, and those who are faithful: "God...has engaged to grant pardon by means of repentance, saying to the people: 'repent thee and I will save thee'; and again 'I live, saith the Lord, and I will have repentance rather than death'" (*On Repentance* 4.1).[47]

ORIGEN

The genius of Origen (c. 185–254) opened a new era in early Christian reflection.[48] As with most issues dealt with in depth by Origen, it is difficult to state precisely what he thought and said about the Eucharist. He deals with it occasionally, scattered across his multifaceted output. As Henri Crouzel explains, with reference to his thought on the Eucharist, "Origen gives to the gospel texts on which he is commenting a whole spectrum of meanings, in which those which express the real presence are cheek by jowl with very different ones."[49] Nevertheless, in his *Commentary on Matthew*, he articulates a view that reflects the need for baptism and faith on the one hand, and the defilement that comes from lack of faith on the other:

> It is not the meat but the conscience of him who eats with doubt which defiles him that eateth, for "he that doubteth is condemned if he eat, because he eateth not of faith,"[50] and if nothing is pure to him who is defiled and unbelieving, not in itself, but because of his defilement and unbelief, so that which is sanctified by the word of God and prayer does not, in its own nature, sanctify him who uses it, for, if this were so, it would sanctify even him who eats unworthily of the bread of the Lord. (*Commentary on Matthew* XI.14)[51]

The traditional insistence on authentic Christian faith as an essential requirement for the strengthening that comes from the reception of the sacrament continues to be the determining factor. It appears that Origen was not interested in whether the participant in the eucharistic celebration believed or was not guilty of sin. If that was the case, then participation in the sacrament would have no strengthening effect. Only with the right disposition would the sacrament be of saving use to the well-prepared believer. As Crouzel points out, there is a lack of a formulated distinction between the saving effects of the sacrament in itself, and condition of the recipient necessary for such effects, but these distinctions (*ex opere operato* and *ex opere operantis*) developed later in the tradition.[52]

An important development in emerging Christianity took place late in the fourth century. A collection of texts was formally accepted as Christian Sacred Scripture. The matter had been debated for some centuries. Origen had played a major role in determining what writings were certainly Scripture, possibly Scripture, and definitely not Scripture. The authority of Athanasius, and his Easter Letter of 367, designated the twenty-seven books of our present New Testament as the only canonical books.[53] Once these books were accepted in the East and the West as canonical Scriptures, they gained great authority. Gospel texts and the Letters of Paul had been widely used in the earlier writings, but now the text could be used as an authoritative voice. This led to the increasing impact of biblical texts on the developing Tradition.

AUGUSTINE

Augustine (354–430) was the most influential of the Latin fathers. Augustine's *Homilies on the Gospel of John* LXII reflects on John 13:26–31: the gift of the morsel to Judas and its consequences.[54] Augustine uses Luke 22:19–21 to develop a chronology that excludes Judas from participating in the reception of the body of Christ (LXII.3), but he is still concerned by the fact that some listeners may be disturbed because Jesus shows such goodness to the betrayer. He therefore asks the question: How is this possible? He responds by stating the principle that "the point of special importance is, not the character of the thing that is given, but of him to whom it is given" (LXII.1). In the guise of a friend, an enemy has come to the Table of the Lord (see John 13:18). In that situation, the word of 1 Corinthians 11:27 can be applied to Judas, without any reference to its original context: "Whoever, therefore, eats the bread or drinks the cup of the Lord in an unworthy manner will be answerable for the body and blood of the Lord." The tradition of using 1 Corinthians 11:27–28, without reference to its origins as a Pauline attack on the arrogant wealthy in Corinth, has become part of the tradition. In a brilliant reading of Jesus's self-gift to the unworthy Judas, Augustine comments: "And why was the bread given to the traitor, but as an evidence of the grace he had treated with ingratitude." Augustine's original Latin is stunning in its clarity and beauty: *Quid erat autem panis traditori datus, nisi demonstratio cui gratiae fuisset ingratus.* Jesus's unconditional love for the betrayer remains in place (LXII.1).

A creative reading of the Johannine episode continues, as Judas's betrayal is interpreted as delivering up Christ for the "business" of his own gain, whereas the true significance of the event is Christ delivering himself up for "the business of our redemption." In the end, Judas's actions have no power in themselves, "because He who wills it has all the power" (LXII.4). Even the reference to Judas's role as the keeper of the money-box leads Augustine to explain: "The Lord, therefore, had also a money-box, where He kept the offerings of believers, and distributed to the necessities of his own, and to others who were in need" (LXII.5). The theme of care for the marginalized, so consistent across these early centuries, remains in place. Jesus's proclamation of the arrival of the hour for the glorification of the Son of Man, as a consequence of Judas's departure into the night (John 13:31–32) draws the remark, "The day therefore uttered speech unto the day, that is, Christ did so to His faithful disciples, that they might hear and love him as His followers; and the night showed knowledge unto the night, that is, Judas did so to the unbelieving Jews, that they might come as His persecutors" (LXII.6).

CYRIL OF ALEXANDRIA

Cyril of Alexandria (387–444), the successor of Athanasius, the paragon of orthodoxy in Alexandria, has been described as "though unlikely to have been a pleasant man to know, was more than simply an unscrupulous party boss."[55] Diarmaid MacCulloch claims that his eucharistic theology exemplifies this:

> When he contemplated his Saviour Jesus Christ, he could see only God offering his presence to sinful humanity, especially every time the Church offered Christ's flesh and blood in the bread and wine of the Eucharist.[56]

Cyril continues Augustine's interpretation of John 13:26–27, crediting Jesus Christ with a remarkable act of love, and Judas with the rejection of that love. As with Augustine, Cyril points out that Satan's possession of Judas in verse 27 is not the result of Jesus's gift of the morsel, but the failure of the recipient (*Commentary on John* 13:26–27):

> When all love was perfectly shown to him, and nothing at all was lacking of the things that are considered to imply a disposition to confer honor, he still clung to the same pursuits, never correcting his evil intentions by repentance, never turning his heart away from its lawless designs, never weeping in bitter sorrow for the evils he had dared even to conceive. (*Commentary on John* 13:26–27)[57]

Cyril adds to the Augustinian presentation of the unconditional love of Jesus, met by the failure of Judas, a note of possible repentance ("never correcting," "never turning," "never weeping"). Unlike Augustine, he makes no use of 1 Corinthians 11:27–28 to declare Judas as "unworthy," nor does he refer to the complex narrative of Luke 22:14–38 to deny the possibility that the morsel given to Judas was not eucharistic. Of course, he may have taken that for granted, but he does state that "all love was perfectly shown to him," and that Jesus's disposition was "to confer honor" and "the blessing he received from Christ" (*Commentary on John* 13:26–27).

There is a breadth in Cyril's treatment of the question of one's worthiness to access the Table of the Lord. The theme receives a fine expression in his discussion of "the mystery" of Jesus's rejection of Mary Magdalene's desire to cling on to him in John 20:17.[58] Cyril asks why the fact of Jesus's having not yet ascended into heaven should be sufficient reason "for those who love him not to be able to touch his holy body" (*Commentary on John* 20:17).[59] There can be no question of the pollution of his divine nature. Indeed, "there are many different purposes for our Savior's advent, but this one is the most important and is revealed by his own words: 'I have come to call not the righteous but sinners to repentance.'"[60] Cyril looks back to the time of Jesus's ministry, pointing out that during that period, part of the divine economy, he mixed with sinners, using the examples of the sinful woman who anointed Jesus's feet with her hair (see Luke 7:37–38) and the touching of the woman with the flow of blood (see Luke 8:43–44).

At that time, according to the *oeconomia*, the impure and polluted in both body and mind could touch the holy flesh of Christ our Savior and enjoy every blessing from it. But once he has fulfilled the *oeconomia* for us, and has endured the cross itself and death on the cross, come to life, and shown his nature to be stronger than death, he prevents those who approach him and does not let them touch his holy flesh.

The death, resurrection, and ascension of Jesus open a new era in the divine economy: the period of the Spirit. Looking back to Moses's command that no uncircumcised person could eat the slaughtered lamb (Exod 12:48), Cyril sees the slaughtered lamb as a figure of the "holy body of Christ." Thus, he insists, "While we are still uncircumcised, that is, impure, we must not touch the holy body, but rather we must be made pure by the circumcision that is the Spirit." Mary Magdalene must wait, therefore, until Jesus returns to the Father and sends the Spirit (see John 20:17; 16:7). In a rich development of the consistent teaching of the tradition that baptism and faith are required for access to the eucharistic table, Cyril concludes,

> This is a type of the churches. Accordingly we keep from the holy table even those who understand the divinity of Christ and have confessed their faith (that is, the catechumens) when

> they have not been enriched with the Holy Spirit. After all, he does not dwell in those who are not yet baptized.... That is why to those who wish to partake in the mystical blessing, the ministers of the divine mysteries announce, "The holy things to holy people," teaching that participation in the holy things is appropriate for those who are sanctified by the Spirit.

Not only does Cyril continue the tradition of a call for conversion and repentance as a necessary element in the experience of coming to "touch the body of Jesus," but he locates it specifically in the institution that, by his time, had been instituted precisely for these purposes: the catechumenate.

A cursory reading of some representatives of the growing Christian Tradition makes it clear that the Church understood the holiness and forgiveness available in the gift of the Eucharist. Yet the forgiveness communicated to the participants through their "remembering" the death and resurrection of Jesus depended on their prior insertion into that mysterious action of God for humankind in and through his Son: baptism. But baptism was not the only requirement. The baptized had to commit themselves to an ongoing life of faith and commitment, recognizing their sinfulness, turning to God in repentance, forgiving others, as they were forgiven.[61] By Cyril's time, this process had been institutionalized in the catechumenate. The Eucharist is a celebration of forgiveness for those who recognize their needs and failures, and turn to Jesus Christ.

LEO THE GREAT, FULGENTIUS OF RUSPE, AND MAXIMUS THE CONFESSOR

Three later figures from the tradition indicate that this approach to forgiveness was one of the core elements in Christian life and practice. They all come from conflicted times. Leo the Great (DOB unknown–461 CE) witnessed the beginning of the invasion of the Roman Empire, right to the city gates, of nations from beyond the Empire. At the heart of his ministry was deep concern for the unity of the far-reaching presence of Christianity, especially in its unity of faith and practice. He preserves the essential element of forgiveness in that tradition of unity, faith, and practice, insisting on the importance of forgiveness:

All the more wonderful is the mercy of God towards us, because Christ died not just for the just or the holy but for the wicked and the impious. And though the divine nature could not admit the sting of death, by being born from us he took what he could offer for us. (*Tractatus de Passione Domini* 59.8)

The victory of the cross is denied to none of the weak; there is no man who cannot be helped by the prayer of Christ. For if his prayer aided the multitudes who raged against him, how much more does it help those who turn to him? (*Tractatus de Passione Domini* 66.3)[62]

Born in North Africa and deeply influenced by Augustine, Fulgentius, bishop of Ruspe (c. 465–c.533), was an only son who resisted family objections to embrace monastic life. Adopting an aggressive "orthodoxy," he shifted across North Africa and Italy to find a location where he could live and minister without persecution from Arian Christians. A very learned figure, he was a dedicated and widely admired charismatic preacher. His understanding of Eucharist and the Christian life was nourished by his use of the Word of God in the Scriptures.

The spiritual building up of the body of Christ is achieved through love. As St. Peter says, "Like living stones you are built into a spiritual house to be a holy priesthood, offering spiritual sacrifices acceptable to God through Jesus Christ." There can be no more effective way to pray for this spiritual growth than for the Church, itself Christ's body, to make the offering of his body and blood in the sacramental form of blood and wine. "For the cup we drink is a participation in the blood of Christ and the bread we break is a participation in the body of Christ. Because there is one loaf we who are many are one body, since we share the same bread." (*Ad Monimum* II.1, citing 1 Pet 2:5–6 and 1 Cor 10:16–17)

In his *De Fide ad Petrum*, he applies these thoughts to Eucharist as a celebration of forgiveness:

The holy Catholic church continually offers the sacrifice of bread and wine in faith and charity throughout the whole world. For

> in those carnal victims [animals in Temple sacrifice] the flesh and blood of Christ were prefigured, the flesh which he who was without sin was to offer for our sins, the blood which he was to pour out for the forgiveness of our sins. In this sacrifice, however, there is thanksgiving for and commemoration of the flesh of Christ which he has offered for us and the blood which the same God has poured out for us. (*De Fide ad Petrum* 62)[63]

The later post-Chalcedonian hero of the Eastern Church, Maximus the Confessor (550–662) shares this sentiment: "Nothing is so dear and loved by him as when men turn to him with true repentance." Like Athanasius and Cyril of Alexandria, Leo the Great, and Fulgentius of Ruspe, Maximus starts from the fundamental truth of the reconciliation of sins that flow from incarnation, initiating the possibility that humankind might realize its divine potential:

> Not only did he heal our diseases with his miracles, and sinless, pay our debt for us by his death like a guilty man. It was also his desire that we should become like himself in love of men and in perfect mutual charity, and he taught us this in many ways.
>
> He called sinners, sought out the lost sheep, rejoiced over one sinner who repented, was a Good Samaritan, the father of the prodigal son, and left a hundred sheep in the wilderness to find one lost sheep. He invited all who were heavily burdened to come to him.
>
> After teaching divine righteousness and goodness, he commanded, "Be holy, be perfect, be merciful as your heavenly Father is merciful," and "Forgive and it shall be forgiven you," and "whatever you wish that men would do to you, do so to them" (*Letter* 11; *PG* XCI.454–55, 256–57).[64]

The survey of two New Testament documents (1 Cor 5 and Heb 6), the apostolic fathers and the apologists, into the flowering of the biblically inspired great patristic traditions, reflects a broadly consistent teaching: what was required for admission to the eucharistic table was not sinless perfection but faith in Christ, demonstrated by baptism, a consciousness of sinfulness, and the need for repentance.[65] As time went by, baptism itself demanded a period of repentance and forgiveness that took place in the Catechumenate.[66] John Chryssavgis, in his study of repentance and confession in the Orthodox Tradition, suggests that from the beginning of Christianity, before an established order of confession (tenth century), the decisive acts of repentance and forgiveness took place at the eucharistic celebration: "The supreme act of communion is the eucharist, the communal sharing of the bread and wine, symbolizing sacramentally the reconciliation yet to come and the reconciliation already achieved in the here and now."[67]

THE WORD OF GOD FADES FROM THE SCENE

Risking superficiality in assessing a unique period of Christian life, thought, practice, and artistic expression, the biblically inspired reflections on Christian discipline surrounding the Eucharist gradually began to dissipate in the West, once the turning point of the coronation of Charlemagne took place (800).[68] The West and the East were separated and the chaos of the steady collapse of the Roman Empire was brought to a halt. Politically, the unity generated by Charlemagne and subsequent Western Christian emperors led to conflict between the authority of the Roman papacy and the secular princes. A more juridical, and less biblical, theological, and sacramental self-understanding of Christianity began to develop. The development of a structured hierarchical Church, following the secular models of the time, came to a head in the eleventh century. It is associated with the reforming figure of Pope Gregory VII (1073–85). The authority of the pope over the secular princes was dramatically acted out in the submission of Henry VII (Holy Roman Emperor) to Gregory VII at Canossa in 1077.

The conflicts between the secular and religious powerful authorities, acted out at Canossa, needed to be addressed,[69] but they brought consequences. A more juridical and hierarchical Catholicism emerged, accompanied by an insistence on what was right and wrong, along with disciplinary processes that kept the people subservient to ecclesiastical hierarchy.[70] Great achievements continued in the medieval period with scholars, saints, and artists. Its richness can be *read* in representatives like Thomas Aquinas, *heard* in the splendor of the musical rendition of biblical texts in Gregorian chant, and *seen* in the glass windows of the great medieval churches of Europe.[71] Yet a warm familiarity with the biblical Word of God, so dominant in the patristic period, faded.

Legal traditions supplanted the breadth of vision that came from deep reflection on the Word of God.

A further drift away from a sound use of biblical traditions emerged from the Council of Trent (1545–63), called to guide the Roman tradition in its response to the Protestant Reformation. There were many Catholic doctrines and practices that could not be found in the Bible. The reformers rejected such beliefs and practices as the institution of the priesthood, many Marian teachings, the seven sacraments, the papacy, and the real presence of the crucified and risen Jesus in the celebration of the Eucharist. These doctrines were not found in the Word of God of the Old and New Testaments. In its third session (1546) in its decree on the reception of Scripture and Tradition, the council responded by teaching that there were two sources of revelation: Tradition and Scripture (DS 1501).[72] It was true that many doctrines and practices of the Catholic Church could not be found in the Bible, but they could be found in the Tradition. If a belief or a practice of the Catholic Church could not be found in the Bible, the authentic Tradition of the Church could be called on as the source of such revelations. The dominant opinion was that the revelation found in the Catholic Tradition was superior to the revelation found in the Bible. In 1870, this assessment of Tradition and Scripture was repeated in the Constitution on Revelation (*Dei Filius*) at Vatican I.[73] The use of the Sacred Scriptures in the life and thinking of the Church faded further.

As is well known, one of the motivating forces that led the Augustinian monk Martin Luther to cry out for a "reform" of Catholic Tradition was Rome's increasing focus on the use of what he regarded as "worldly authority" and the dramatic loss of contact with the demands of the Word of God and early Christian traditions. His teaching on the Eucharist reflects his concerns.[74] Luther's understanding of the so-called words of institution shifted the focus away from what happened to the species of the bread and wine (so central to Catholic teaching) to what the Lord's Supper does for the believer. As expressed in the Evangelical Lutheran Confession of Faith, "Whoever believes these words [the words of institution] has exactly what they say and what they express, namely, forgiveness of sin."[75] Whatever the Catholic theological tradition response concerning the effect of the words of institution on the elements, Luther accurately reflected the great Tradition of the Church catholic in his understanding of the Eucharist as a celebration of forgiveness.

The Christian Churches, especially the Catholic Church, understandably developed a defensive approach to what has been called the Enlightenment and the Age of Reason. As the Rationalists claimed that the only guaranteed "truths" were those that could be proved by experience and experimentation, an affirmation of many traditional "doctrines" was widespread. The more subtle problem of the emergence of a scholarly critical interpretation of the Bible in the nineteenth century, sometimes aggressively anti-Christian, generated a further Catholic dissipation in the use of the Scriptures in the life of the Church.

The emerging understanding of the Eucharist across this period, and the regulations surrounding its practice, exemplified this. The Roman Rite was gradually imposed on all medieval practices, the active participation of the laity ceased, the bishop and the priest took over the role of the corporate celebration, offering the sacrifice for the people, and often especially for the spiritual benefit of individuals, who did not have to be present. The "private Mass" evolved to become a feature of the Western Church, with its associated dangers of the "sale" of Masses and other disorders.[76] The laypeople withdrew from a *celebration* and *adored* the consecrated bread. The elevation of the host by the priest became more important than the people's reception. Despite their incredible architectural beauty, the Gothic churches and cathedrals separated the priest from the people. A physical gap existed between the celebrating priest with his back to the people and the silent inactive faithful. This was further accentuated by the use of the rood screen. The biblical notion of eucharistic "presence," generated by "memory," was superseded by the philosophical/theological notion of "transubstantiation."[77] A legal understanding of the Eucharist, divorced from the New Testament message of a loving self-gift that generates unity and forgiveness among fragile believers was challenged by Vatican II (see, e.g, *SC* 5–46, especially the articulation of the fundamental principles for reform in no. 7), but many aspects of it (e.g., the role of the priest, the importance of adoration for many, the insistence on Latin as the determining linguistic tradition in all translations, the extreme reluctance of Roman authorities to allow the inculturation of liturgical practices) remain alive within contemporary Catholicism.[78]

In its Decree on the Eucharist (1551), the Council of Trent (1543–63) indicated that the exclusion of all who might be unworthy of access to the eucharistic table is motivated by Paul's warning not to divide the community between the wealthy and the less fortunate (1 Cor 11:27–29). The passage is cited with the descriptor: "as we read in the Apostle's fearful words" (*formidinis verba*) (DS 1646). Those "fearful words" have lost their biblical and theological significance as a warning of those who are creating division in "the one body" and are used as a legal instrument against a person or group excluded as "sinners," often causing discrimination and division in that same body.

Catholic Tradition on marriage is another example of the enduring legal processes of Catholic thought and practice. The patristic era, especially under the influence of Augustine, saw marriage as a secular reality. It was never considered as "a Sacrament," that is, a place where human signs and symbols communicated God's grace. As such, marriage was understood as a necessary secondary element in the life of Christians, when compared with the riches promised by God's kingdom.[79] It was a secular reality that ensured the birth of children and a more stable society, especially in legally protecting women against sexual and social abuse.

The medieval period was also ambiguous, as the scholastics continued to have difficulty understanding how marriage conferred grace. Peter Abelard (1079–1142) was one of many distinguished medieval theologians who speculated about the sacraments. Arguing in favor of seven sacraments, he groups marriage with baptism, confirmation, Eucharist, and the anointing of the sick, but he can still write, "Among them [these sacraments] there is one that does not avail unto salvation and yet is the sacrament of a weighty matter, namely matrimony, for to bring a wife home is not meritorious for salvation, but it is allowed for salvation's sake because of incontinence" (*Epitome theologiae Christianae* 28; PL CLXXVIII:1738). The authority of Peter Lombard (1100–1160) and his *Four Books of Sentences* established the Catholic teaching of seven sacraments,[80] but nothing was determined by the Church itself until 1439. During the attempt to restore unity with the Eastern Churches at the Council of Florence, the *Decree for the Armenians* established agreement on seven sacraments. For the first time, the Catholic magisterium stated that marriage contains grace and communicates grace to those who receive it worthily (DS 1327).

This position was formally canonized at the Council of Trent.[81] In 1520, Martin Luther, in his *De captivitate Babylonica ecclesiae praeludium*, rejected marriage as a sacrament, as it has no founding moment in the Scriptures. This opinion was endorsed by the subsequent Lutheran creed in the *Augsburg Confession* (1530). The reformers also approved the practice of divorce as a lesser of two evils. Trent expressly defines that marriage is a sacrament, instituted by Christ (using Eph 5:25, 32), conferring grace, in its *Doctrine on the Sacrament of Matrimony* of 1563 (DS 1799–1800). The council fathers condemned all who rejected this teaching in the first canon attached to this decree (DS 1801). In the fifth of these canons, they condemned as heretical all who claimed that a marriage could be dissolved (DS 1805).[82] The notion of marriage as a sacrament, leading to centuries of ecclesiastical interventions on all aspects of married life, does not belong to the great Catholic Tradition. It has its origins in the sixteenth century, and current Roman Catholic legislation, originating in the conflicts of that time, continues to show very little "forgiveness."

CONCLUSION

From our present vantage point, the fading of the rich biblical reflections that had directed Christian thought and practice for most of the first Christian millennium has led to an impoverishment of major elements in the Christian Tradition. One of them was an understanding of the Eucharist as a celebration of forgiveness. There are many reasons for this, not all of them negative. However, the many voices that inspired the thought and practice of the Christian Tradition in the West and East tended to disappear. The East continued to develop along its own way, splintering into a number of patriarchates, separating itself from the increasing centralization of the West. The focus of the West on Rome was not without its dramatic reversals. The shift of the papal seat to Avignon, the consequent confusion over a rightful papacy, and the schisms associated with it from the fourteenth till the sixteenth century were the most spectacular. However, the problem was generated by a lack of agreement about ecclesiastical discipline and where it was to be located. The critical debates over Conciliarism were basically about *authority* (pope or council).[83] All of this had its tortured place in the history of Western Christianity and played its part in the emergence of the reformers.

However, an important element present in the earlier biblical, patristic, and liturgical traditions disappeared in these critical historical moments: the gift of forgiveness. A focus on forgiveness may well have led to a different model of Church than that produced by the Councils of Pisa (1409), Constance (1414–18), Basel (1431–49), and the Fifth Lateran Council (1512–17). But that was impossible at the time. It had been replaced by a carefully argued and articulated legal approach to the mysteries, administered by a hierarchically structured and sacramentally ordained male leadership. The profound dependence on the Scriptures, so obvious in what we have shared from the *Didache* (early second century CE) to Maximus the Confessor (seventh century CE), had almost completely disappeared.

CHAPTER 4

Eucharist as a Celebration of Forgiveness

Current debates surrounding eucharistic practice within the Roman Catholic Tradition swirl around differences of opinion on what is—and what is not—Catholic doctrine. The problems surround "practice," not the core belief that the Eucharist is the source and summit of Christian life and practice (*LG* 11; *SC* 10), "so great a work" that Jesus Christ is present in the minister, the sacred species, the Word, and the community that prays and sings (*SC* 7). The so-called "doctrinal" problems are associated with the question of who should be admitted to the table. For some, what the Church decided about its eucharistic discipline at the sixteenth-century Council of Trent is immutable doctrine, and no one is permitted to suggest any rethinking, much less alteration. The same is claimed for decisions taken at Trent regarding the discipline surrounding marriage and the family, even though the sacrament of marriage was formally declared one of the seven sacraments only at the council itself.

Pope Francis has stepped into these debates with magisterial vigor. At a gathering of the Italian Church in Florence on November 10, 2015, he insisted,

> We are not living in an era of change but a change of era. Before the problems of the Church it is not useful to search for solutions in conservatism or fundamentalism, in the restoration of obsolete conduct and forms that no longer have the capacity of being significant culturally. Christian doctrine is not a closed system incapable of generating questions, doubts,

> interrogatives—but is alive, knows being unsettled, enlivened. It has a face that is not rigid, it has a body that moves and grows, it has soft flesh: it is called Jesus Christ.[1]

That gathering had featured a reading of the Beatitudes from the Gospel of Matthew (Matt 5:1–12). The pope pleads for a return to the spirit of Jesus and the Gospel: "If the church does not assume the sentiments of Jesus, it is disoriented, it loses its sense. The beatitudes, in the end, are the mirror in which we see ourselves, that which permits us to know if we are walking on the right path: it is a mirror that does not lie."[2] The biblical and patristic reflections presented to this point in our study are an attempt to respond to the call of Pope John XXIII and Vatican II to gaze more consistently into the mirror of the face of Jesus Christ, convinced that it does not lie. The process of *ressourcement*, a return to the sources of the Christian faith, penetrates two thousand years of gradual cultural and disciplinary practice. But Pope Francis has laid down the gauntlet: "As pastors may you not be preachers of complex doctrine, but pronouncers of Christ, dead and resurrected for us. Aim for the essential *kerygma*."[3]

THE *KERYGMA*

The heated interventions that mark Paul's Letter to the Galatians (see 1:6–9; 3:1–5; 4:8–11; 4:31—5:1; 5:7–12) reflect the anxious and angry mind and heart of someone who senses that his preaching of Jesus's death and resurrection was being rendered vain. But it addresses a critical situation in Galatia, and we have no information of what effect Paul's intervention may or may not have had.[4] There are two canonical letters to a community generating similar passion, although for different reasons: 1 and 2 Corinthians. The Corinthian correspondence provides evidence of Paul's troubled relationship over a lengthy period with an early Christian community that he founded. We have already had occasion to consider Paul's instructions to them, arising from various reports that generated 1 Corinthians that seem to be coming to Paul at Ephesus in the mid-50s CE. Many have suggested that the canonical 2 Corinthians is a collection of up to five different letters, although a good case can be made for it being a single, if rather extraordinary, utterance.[5] Whatever the truth about that question, the tensions and differences of opinion between Paul and his new Christians in Corinth generated considerable pain, anger, anxiety, and the need for continual intervention from the Apostle of the Gentiles. Although we have only one side of this conversation, there were clearly communications from members of the Corinthian Church to Paul, not all of them friendly! There were even some in Corinth who questioned Paul's apostolic authority (see 2 Cor 2:1—7:4; 10:1—12:21). It must have been an extraordinary young Church, working out its newly found Christian way at the crossroads between East and West.[6] There were no doubt failures among members of the community to measure up to Paul's preaching and his ideals, met sometimes by a rather irascible Paul. Nevertheless, in opening his second letter to them, he writes,

> Blessed be the God and Father…of mercies and the God of all consolation, who consoles us in all our affliction, so that we may be able to console those who are in any affliction with the consolation with which we ourselves are consoled by God. For just as the sufferings of Christ are abundant for us, so also our consolation is abundant through Christ. (2 Cor 1:3–5)

Paul yearns for Christians who recognize what God has done for them in the death and resurrection of Jesus Christ. He reaches out to them in an act of consolation, administering the consolation he has received from God. He asks the members of the community, in their own turn, to manifest the mercy and consolation shown them in Jesus Christ in their mercy and consolation for others. He delivered the same message in his first letter, as he exhorted them to give themselves unconditionally for others, "in memory" of Jesus until he comes again (1 Cor 11:24–26).[7] The very existence of the Corinthian correspondence indicates that Paul never "gives up" on his failing community.[8] He is stern with them: "Should I commend you? In this matter I do not commend you!" (1 Cor 11:22). But he does not abandon them. In imitation of Christ (see 11:1), he loves them, forgives them, and writes to them in his own hand that they will be ready for the day of the Lord: "Let anyone be accursed who has no love for the Lord. Our Lord, come! The grace of the Lord Jesus be with you. My love be with all of you in Christ Jesus" (16:22–24).

Paul's *kerygma* is clear, as we have seen. The Corinthians could not claim to be "the body of the Lord" (the Church) as long as they did not "discern the body" (equally Church) in lesser creatures, especially the poor and abandoned, but Paul has heard that the Corinthians were excluding them from the eucharistic table (1 Cor 11:17–22). The Church is called to recognize that it finds its very reason for existence in the needs of all who look to the Lord's Table for oneness with him, and for oneness in the community itself. Only then will it meet the Pauline requirements for a Christian Eucharist. This is the meaning of Paul's words about examining one's worthiness in 1 Corinthians 11:27–28. The care and affection that Paul demonstrates, based on the love and care of Jesus Christ, is rooted in the Father who sent him (see 1 Cor 1:3–5). The word *forgiveness* is not found, but Paul's relationship with his fractious community is surely one marked by forgiveness.

In order to make this point, Paul goes back to the *kerygma* that he has received and has taught them (11:23). He tells the story of the night when Jesus was betrayed to remind the Corinthians that Jesus did not accept the suffering that was his destiny in some passive way. It was not something that was "for himself," but "for you" (v. 24). Fully aware that he had been called to a radical loyalty to both God and to his fellow human beings, the experience of Calvary was embraced to produce fruits that would save the world (see Rom 3:21–26; 5:12–21; Phil 2:5–11). So must it also be for those who are caught up in the "rhythm" of Eucharist, a rhythm that touches both a eucharistic celebration and a eucharistic life. Disciples of Jesus are summoned to lives marked by a deep awareness that we are united to Jesus, to God, and to the rest of humankind. Like Jesus, Christians live eucharistic lives that both recall the saving events that took place in the life and death of Jesus, and indicate that they are prepared to be victims, breaking their bodies and spilling their blood for others. In this way, Paul comments, they will recall the Lord's death until he comes again (see 11:26).

The eucharistic liturgy is the source and the summit of a eucharistic life given without limit (see *LG* 11; *SC* 10). Such was the quality of the life of Jesus: it *must* mark the lives of all his disciples, and his Church, as they live henceforth by and in him. The celebration of the Eucharist is the Church's fundamental and life-giving "memory" of the death and resurrection of Jesus. As in the Jewish theological tradition, the "memory" of the death and resurrection of Jesus "makes present" what is remembered (see 1 Cor 11:24, 25; Luke 22:19; see also 1 Cor 11:26). *Only* in the death and resurrection of Jesus is God's saving action at work. Sins are forgiven, and the free gift of God's saving love is dispensed through the unconditional, loving, and obedient response of Jesus to God. Through no "merit" of our own, through no "worthiness" that we Christians can generate, do we *receive* God's free gift of pardon. Eucharist, in so far as it renders present the reality and the fruits of Jesus's death and resurrection, *must* be a celebration of forgiveness. The Eucharist is the critical location within the practice of Christian life, where hope and reconciliation are encountered, as God gifts his beloved creation with the presence of his Son. The forgiveness celebrated at the Eucharist is a gift of Jesus Christ, Son of the Father of mercies, and the God of all consolation (see 2 Cor 1:3).

Paul's narrative reporting events that had developed into *kerygma*, even before his time, is our earliest witness to a theology of the Eucharist. The narrative of 1 Corinthians 11:23–25, told in conjunction with Paul's concerns about the arrogance of the wealthy who disregard the lowly, communicates a theological point of view. The development of the primitive Church's theology continues in the later narratives of the Gospels that appeared between 70–100 CE. Mark, Matthew, Luke, and John do not "tell a story" merely to put the past on record. Despite the different times and locations of their origins, these inspired books from our Christian Sacred Scripture converge around two fundamental teachings that should be *normative* in the Christian Tradition:

1. The Pauline insistence on the "one body" of the Christian community as essential understanding and participation in the "one bread," which is the Eucharist (1 Cor 10:16–17), continues in the accounts of the multiplication of the loaves and fishes in the Gospels of Mark (6:31–44; 8:1–10) and Matthew (14:13–21; 15:32–39). The same call to unity, a gathering of both Jew and Gentile around the Table of the Lord drives the Markan and Matthean twofold telling of the story of the multiplication of the loaves and fishes (Mark 6:31–44; 8:1–10; Matt 14:13–21; 15:32–39). Although framed differently, the Lukan use of the literary form of a farewell discourse in his account of Jesus's final meal with his disciples (Luke 22:14–38) is directed to a Gentile world. Luke assures his audience that fragile disciples were solemnly commissioned to be apostles who would strengthen their brothers (see v. 32).

Jesus confers on them, just as the Father has conferred on him, a kingdom, "so that you may eat and drink at my table in my kingdom" (vv. 29–30). Jesus will be there with them, "as one who serves" (v. 27). As he told Theophilus, he is telling this story "so that you may know the truth... about which you have been instructed" (1:4). Although more succinct, the Johannine Jesus, on the night before he died, gave a new example (John 13:15) and a new commandment (vv. 34–35): the sign of their being his disciples will be their love for one another. Such love will instruct "the world" (see v. 35; 17:21, 23, 25–26).

2. All four evangelists, each in his own way, reports that Jesus's final meal with his disciples, the night before he died, was the darkest night in the history of Christianity (Mark 14:17–31; Matt 26:17–35; Luke 22:14–38; John 13:1–38). It was the night one of his disciples, Judas, betrayed him; another of them, Simon Peter, denied him three times, while everyone else deserted him. As each evangelist, using his own sources, examines the living memory of earliest Christian Tradition, reports these *facts*, and develops his unique eucharistic story, we are aware that Jesus shared this foundational meal with sinners (see *DV* 19). In his own inimitable fashion, Luke stresses Jesus's care for the sinner as he searches out the two disciples who have left the city of Jerusalem for Emmaus, touches their minds and hearts at a eucharistic meal, and leads them home (Luke 24:13–35). On the same night at another meal in the city of Jerusalem, he commissions his failed disciples to preach repentance and the forgiveness of sins "to all nations, beginning from Jerusalem" (24:36–49).

There can be no gainsaying these origins. They are etched forever into Christian memory and its storytelling. This *kerygma* must be formative of all subsequent eucharistic thought and practice in the Christian Churches: the Eucharist is a celebration of forgiveness. Jesus's forgiveness is implicit in all the accounts of his final meal with his failing disciples. In the Gospel of Matthew, it is rendered explicit in Jesus's words over the cup: "poured out for many for the forgiveness of sins" (Matt 26:28) and in Jesus's words to Simon in the Gospel of

Luke: "Simon, Simon, listen! Satan has demanded to sift all of you like wheat, but I have prayed for you that your own faith may not fail; and you, when once you have turned back, strengthen your brothers" (Luke 22:31–32). It lies at the heart of the transformation of Jesus's disciples in the Gospel of John. At the moment ("now"), they cannot understand what Jesus is saying and doing. They can only be described as obtuse failures. But a time will come ("afterwards"), when they will come to believe that Jesus is the exquisite revelation of God's love and forgiveness (John 13:7, 19, 36).

The promise of Jesus's forgiveness ("once you have turned back") is acted out in the Easter experiences reported in the walk to Emmaus and the subsequent commissioning of the disciples in Jerusalem: "Repentance and forgiveness of sins is to be proclaimed in his name to all nations, beginning from Jerusalem. You are witnesses of these things" (Luke 24:47–48). An awareness of God's gracious gift of the Eucharist, including the gift of God's forgiveness, within the developing Christian Tradition, comes from the growing understanding of the immensity of the love of God manifested in the death and resurrection of Jesus.[9] The symbols of bread broken and wine poured out communicated this message powerfully. The richness of the biblical tradition nourished the early and patristic eras. Already in the New Testament, however, an awareness of the sacredness of God's gifts suggested that conversion, baptism, and repentance were essential for the full participation of the faithful in "the mystery" of the Eucharist. Jesus of Nazareth, his earliest interpreters, and the early Christian centuries desired that all might have access to the nourishment and forgiveness available in the celebration of the Eucharist, but there was an awareness that not everyone was worthy, or ready, for such participation. The recognition of failure, the need for conversion, repentance, and insertion into the "body of Christ," which is the Church, emerged as the crucial criteria for "worthiness."

As the Church became more identified with the Western secular authorities, these deeply theological conditions for insertion into the "body of Christ" faded from the Church's imagination, sacramental practice, and legislation. In a world where adhesion to Christianity was part and parcel of society, a legal tradition emerged that gradually lost touch with the inspiration of the Sacred Scriptures and the Church's liturgical and theological traditions. As we have seen, in the case of its use of 1 Corinthians 11:27–28, Scripture used without reference to its original setting can become "proof texts" often to support legal decisions that have no relation with the founding *kerygma*. These developments were not the result of ill will on the part of the major figures who shaped Christian thought and practice over the second Christian millennium. No doubt the perennial problem of human ambition and the imposition of secular criteria played their part, but Christianity, both Catholic and Protestant, was caught up in the forces of European history. Regretfully, from our present vantage point, the fading of the rich biblical reflections that had directed Christian thought and practice for most of the first Christian millennium has led to an impoverishment of major elements in the Christian Tradition: one of them was God's gift of forgiveness. Such reflections were replaced by a carefully argued and articulated legal approach to the mysteries, administered by a hierarchically structured and sacramentally ordained male leadership.

THE DOCTRINE OF FORGIVENESS

Forgiveness remains a mark of the contemporary Christian Churches, especially obvious in the sacrament of reconciliation,[10] but its integral role articulated in the founding *kerygma* associated with the celebration of the Eucharist calls for further consideration. There are many ways one could do this, but following the process of *ressourcement*, it may be useful to reach back sixteen hundred years to a moment in the early Church's articulation of its faith. As the Christian centuries pass, the Christian Church's need to preserve and confess the faith that is constitutive of its very existence in the world and society must be preserved. The earliest centuries debated, sometimes heatedly and even violently, how best to confess that faith. Necessary institutions exist to maintain and preserve its integrity, yet to ensure that it is expressed in many and various ways as times, locations, and cultures change. It is sometimes said that the New Testament created more problems than it provided answers. This is not entirely true, but "unresolved questions" were passed on to the early centuries. What was the Church to make of Jesus's and the New Testament's teaching on the Father, the Son, and the Holy Spirit (Matt 28:16–20)? What does it mean to say that Jesus had his origins in God, but took on our flesh, making God known because he is the only Son of the Father (John 1:14–18), like unto us in all things except sin (Heb 4:15), crying out to his Father in anguish as he died, "My God, my God, why have you forsaken me?" (Mark 15:34)? What does Jesus's return to the Father through ascension and the fulfillment of the promised gift of the Holy Spirit Paraclete mean (Luke 24:49; Acts 1:1–11; John 7:39; 14:16–17; 15:26–27; 16:7–11, 12–15; 19:30)? How does the figure of Mary of Nazareth fit into this unfolding of God's design for humankind (Luke 1—2; John 19:25–27; Acts 1:14)?

From these beginnings, especially through the teachings formulated in the great councils of the Church at Nicaea (325), Constantinople (381), Ephesus (431), Chalcedon (451), and Constantinople (553), the doctrines of the Church received their challenging formulation. Most Christians, from the West and the East (with modifications) adhere to what is known as a creed: a statement of what they believe about God, his Son, Jesus Christ, and what God has done for humankind in and through his taking on human flesh as the son of Mary of Nazareth. It is known to us as the Nicene Creed, and most of us recite it publicly as a confession of faith in our Sunday gatherings. The name of the Creed is misleading. It sounds as if it comes from the Council of Nicaea (325). It had its beginning there, but it was forged through troubled conflict and debate over the years between the Council of Nicaea and the Council of Constantinople (431). The full name for the Creed we recite on Sundays is "The Nicene-Constantinopolitan Creed," and it can be dated to 381, the year of the First Council of Constantinople.[11]

Appeal is rightly made to the central role that doctrine must play in the Catholic Tradition, but the danger always exists that disciplines and practices develop over the centuries, responding to challenges that Christianity must necessarily face. In our study so far, we have touched upon the challenge of taking the message of Jesus into the Greco-Roman world, the tendency to move from the Scriptures to a more legal understanding of Christianity in medieval Europe, the further cultural and religious challenges of the Protestant Reformation, the Enlightenment, and its associated age of reason. The Christian Churches have responded to each of these challenges. However, tied to a time, place, as well as philosophical and theological mindset and language of that time and place, the immutable hard-and-fast articulation of beliefs run the risk of tarnishing the splendor of the fundamental doctrines that determine Christianity. Such teaching and associated practices, however useful and important they may have been when they first emerged, can sometimes distort the bedrock doctrines that are the basis of Christian faith.[12]

The same can be said about articulation of the Nicene-Constantinopolitan Creed itself. What we recite in English on Sundays uses a language that has its origins in the Greek of the fifth-century Christian Church. Words like "God," "maker," "Almighty," "heaven and earth," "seen and unseen," "Lord," "Light from Light," "salvation," "came down from heaven," "resurrection," "ascension," "came again," and "sins" are difficult for many of our contemporaries. We must think hard about what we mean by these words, and be prepared to learn from the saints and masters to spell out their fundamental meaning, if we wish to bring them into our daily lives of faith. As Anthony Kelly states, "The creed today promises no free ride. Our beliefs have to be relearned 'by heart' if they are to resonate from within as expressions of ultimate meaning and promise."[13] Learning the Creed "by heart" does not mean rote memory. It calls for a personal, communitarian, and intimate appropriation of all that God has done for the human condition in and through Jesus Christ. It is not a matter of the mind (although it is also that), but a matter of the heart.

Taking our cue from the eucharistic *kerygma* that we have uncovered, the Nicene Creed can guide us in our search for a doctrinal basis for the claim that the Eucharist is a celebration of forgiveness. The Creed affirms our belief in one God, our Father. We confess our Lord Jesus Christ, his Son, and the Holy Spirit, the giver of life. God is Father and Creator; Jesus Christ is one with the Father from all time. He is from the Father, the medium and agent of all creation. Crucial for a eucharistic theology, he took flesh of the Virgin Mary, was crucified, was buried, and rose again "for all and for our salvation." The Holy Spirit, one with the Father and the Son, gives us life and maintains God's presence in "the holy catholic and apostolic Church." Within that Church, "we acknowledge one baptism *and the forgiveness of sins*," as we wait for the resurrection of the dead and the gift of eternal life. Jesus Christ, from the Father, became flesh, was crucified, and rose again. Within the Spirit-directed Christian community, the saving effects of Jesus's death and resurrection continue, especially in baptism and the Eucharist. The Creed affirms access to life in Christ that we receive in baptism, and the ongoing possibility of maintaining that life through the gift of "the forgiveness of sins."

In these time-honored truths, despite the difficulties of their formulation when expressed in a contemporary world, we have a watershed between the *kerygma* that came to us from Jesus Christ and the teaching of our Sacred Scriptures, and all subsequent expressions of Christian faith. It is the bedrock on which subsequent speculation is built.

> It is a classic articulation of faith in the history of self-expression. Its venerable antiquity enables us to reach back, through those sixteen hundred years, through countless baptisms and eucharists, through the confession of successive generations of believers, to those who found in the creed an enduring, focal expression of what they held to and wished to pass on.... To neglect it, to leave it as a more or less unintelligible expression, would be an odd kind of amnesia. Retrieving faith's past is the best resource for facing faith's future.[14]

The Creed's affirmation of faith in the forgiveness of sin is, as we have seen, an integral element in the original *kerygma*, subordinated to the fundamental belief that God is our "Father," an expression that indicates a relationship. A father cares for all his children. God has manifested that care in his incarnate Son, Jesus Christ, who sets out in search of the lost sheep (Luke 15:3–7, Matt 18:12–14; John 10:7–18). The Father will always be found in the darkness, seeking to save his second child, whose anger is separating him from the Father's love. God goes on saying to his lost children, "You are always with me, and all that is mine is yours," asking them to "rejoice, because this brother of yours was dead and has come to life; he was lost and has been found" (Luke 15:31–32). As the Gospel of John puts it, "God so loved the world that he gave his only Son, so that everyone who believes in him may not perish but may have eternal life. Indeed, God did not send the Son into the world to condemn the world, but in order that the world might be saved though him" (3:16–17).[15]

Humankind cannot "pull itself up by its own boot-straps." Lost in a situation of sinfulness to which it has no solution (see Rom 1:18—3:20), the only exit from this darkness must come from a gift of God made known by Jesus Christ (see Rom 3:9–26; John 1:18). The incarnation of the Son of God, whom we know as Jesus Christ (see John 1:14–17), offers humankind a new possibility. Throughout the New Testament and into the earliest teaching of the Church, this mysterious and ultimately inexplicable mystery has been explained in many ways. For Paul, it is a gift of God, handing over his Son to death, revealing God's righteousness, freeing humankind from sin, justifying them by his grace through the redemption found in Christ Jesus, passing over the sin of all those who have faith in Jesus (see Rom 3:21–26).[16] Jesus's response to God is obedience that reverses the disobedience of Adam that generated sin (see Rom 3:21–26). A "new creation" now exists (see 2 Cor 5:17; Gal 6:15), a new era during which humankind can decide to accept the way of Jesus's obedience to the Father, thus experiencing God's graciousness, or choose the way of Adam and remain in a situation of darkness and sin (see Rom 5:12–21). The narratives of Mark, Matthew, and Luke tell of Jesus's embracing the human condition without limitation, and in his death and resurrection manifesting the liberating power of God (see the syntheses of this in Mark 10:45; Matt 20:28; Luke 22:27). For John, Jesus makes known God's saving love (see John 3:16–17), especially in his loving self-gift on the cross, perfecting the task entrusted to him by his Father (see 4:34 and 19:28–30).[17] This revelation can be accepted or refused, but those who accept it are given authority as children of God (see John 1:11–13; 6:25–58). A creed cannot list all these various inspired attempts to explain the inexplicable: new life is made possible for a world trapped in its sinfulness.[18] All it can say is that Jesus, the incarnate Son of the Father, was crucified, was buried, and rose again "for all and for our salvation."

We participate in this new life, freed from sin, through baptism. Plunged into the waters of baptism, we share in Jesus's death and, emerging from those waters, share in the freedom generated by his resurrection. We are united with him in a death like his, and "certainly… united with him in a resurrection like his" (Rom 6:5). "Our old self was crucified with him so that the body of sin might be destroyed, and we might no longer be enslaved to sin" (v. 6). We now have the possibility of being dead to sin and alive to God in Christ Jesus (v. 11). Baptism, however fundamental for our new life, swept up into the perennial saving effects of Jesus's death and resurrection, does not stand alone. Closely linked to baptism are two other sacraments associated with baptism in a trio known in the Catholic Tradition as the sacraments of initiation: confirmation and Eucharist.

As baptism draws the believer into the saving effects of the Father's gift of the Son, confirmation empowers those effects in the life of the believer through the gift of the Spirit.[19] The Christian is caught up into the life of the Trinity. From the very beginning of the biblical story, the Spirit of God is present. The Spirit hovers over the darkness of the deep and the waters before God's creation begins (Genesis 1:1–2). All through the Old Testament and on into Judaism, the Spirit of God is the enduring presence of the invisible God. God may not be obviously present with his people, but the Spirit of God dwells among them, guides them, and can make them holy. Only the Spirit of God can generate the inner transformation that will make the people holy (see Isa 11:2; Ezek 36:26–27).

The story of Pentecost (Acts 2:1–13) describes the universal availability of the Spirit of God, the fruit of Jesus's death and resurrection. The risen Jesus instructs his disciples to stay in the city of Jerusalem "until you have been clothed with the power from on high" (Luke 24:49). Just as thunder and flames had accompanied the establishment of God's people at Sinai (Exod 19:16–22), they return as a new and universal people of God, made up of all the nations, hear the apostolic preaching of the Word of God, despite their different languages and ethnic origins (Acts 2:5–13). John has another way of saying the same thing, associating the gift of the Spirit with "the hour of Jesus." At the cross, the Mother of Jesus and the beloved disciples are instituted as a new family by the crucified Jesus at his "hour" (19:25–27). As Jesus dies, he brings everything, including the Scriptures, to fulfillment (vv. 28–29). He glorifies God and brings to completion his own glorification (see 11:4). He bows his head and "pours down the Spirit" on the infant Church at the foot of the cross (19:30). This is the definitive gift of the Spirit of holiness, accompanied by the water of baptism that flows from Jesus's side (19:34).[20]

The Spirit Paraclete will accompany, teach, throw light upon the powers of evil, strengthen, guide, and enlighten the community of Jesus in the time between his physical presence among us, and his final return (John 14:16–17, 25–26; 15:26–27; 16:7–11, 12–15). For that reason, the baptized and confirmed in the community of Jesus have received the Spirit (Mark 1:8; Luke 3:16) that accompanies us through our journey (John 14:25–26; 16:12–15).

When the Christian community celebrates the Eucharist, it "remembers" these unfathomable gifts of God: the saving gift of his death, resurrection, and ascension, and the ongoing presence of the divine in our lives in the Holy Spirit.[21] There are a number of Eastern Catholic eucharistic traditions who claim that the crucified, risen, and ascended Lord is rendered "present" to the community by means of the prayer that asks the Spirit to descend on the gifts of bread and wine (the *Epiklesis*), rather than in the more Western idea of the pronouncement of the words of institution. This point of view has made an important impact on the renewal of the liturgy after the Second Vatican Council. Roman Catholics now pray,

> You are indeed Holy, O Lord,
> the fount of all holiness.
> Make holy, therefore, these gifts, we pray,
> by sending down your Spirit upon them like the dewfall,
> that they may become for us
> the Body and Blood of our Lord Jesus Christ.
> (*Second Eucharistic Prayer of the Roman Rite*)

> Therefore, O Lord, we humbly implore you:
> by the same Spirit graciously make holy these gifts we have brought to you for consecration,
> that they may become the Body and Blood of your Son our Lord Jesus Christ,
> at whose command we celebrate these mysteries.
> (*Third and Fourth Eucharistic Prayers of the Roman Rite*)

The baptized and confirmed Christian community and each of its believing members are swept up into the mystery of the Trinity—Father, Son, and Holy Spirit—when it celebrates Eucharist. These basic theological truths led the Church, from its earliest days, to insist on baptism as an essential requirement for the fruitful participation in the Eucharist. Only someone who participates in the saving effects of the death, resurrection, and ascension of Jesus, and who has been gifted by the Holy Spirit, can be nourished at this table. The Church has always insisted on "worthiness." Paul has spoken severely to those who celebrate unworthily because their celebrations have generated divisions in the community (1 Cor 11:17–29). The fathers of the Church continued an insistence on worthiness, reflected in recognition of sinfulness and repentance. The Eucharist is not a table open to anyone and everyone. It demands faith in God and Jesus Christ, manifested in baptism, and in the forgiveness of sin.

However, there is another story to be told, found in the biblical saga. It is dominated, from its first pages to its last, by an understanding of a God who frees God's people from the sins and the slavery that their egoism, disobedience, and sinfulness have generated. Creation emerges from chaos (Gen 1:1—2:2), Abraham's obedience generates a people of God (Gen 22:1–18), Israel is liberated from its slavery in Egypt (Exod 14:15—15:21), and then from the slavery of the Babylonian exile (Isa 54:5–14). Freedom and salvation are offered to everyone who turns to God (Isa 55:1–11), and they will be given a new heart and a new spirit (Ezek 36:16–18). God's saving action in and through his Son is the spectacular sequence of this saga. In the darkness of Easter night, the Church prays what it believes:

> This is the night, when Christ broke the prison bars of death and rose victorious from the underworld. Our birth would have been no gain, had we not been redeemed. O wonder of your humble care for us! O love, O charity beyond all telling, to ransom a slave you gave away your son! O truly necessary sin of Adam, destroyed completely by the death of Christ! O happy fault that earned so great, so glorious a Redeemer! O truly blessed night, worthy alone to know the time and the hour when Christ arose from the underworld! This is the night of which it is written: the night shall be as bright as day, dazzling is the night for me, and full of gladness. The sanctifying power of this night dispels wickedness, washes faults away, restores innocence to the fallen, and joy to mourners, drives out hatred, fosters concord, and brings down the mighty. (Easter Vigil, *Exsultet*)[22]

The foundational narratives of all four Gospels make it clear that the Table of the Lord is a place where those who accept their sinfulness can turn in trust and hope (Mark 14:17–31; Matt 26:20–35; Luke 22:14–38, 24:13–49; John 13:1–38). The gift of the Eucharist "remembers" the worst night in Christian history: betrayal, denial, flight, the condemnation of an innocent Jesus, leading to his cruel death the following day. In this "memory," the unimaginable love of God for "his own," without limits, "to the end" (John 13:1; Greek: *eis telos*), is "rendered present" (see v. 19). It is inevitable that all who wish to participate in the eucharistic table will come to that table marked by sin. We are summoned to awe as we witness and experience the loving self-gift of Jesus Christ that takes away our sin. Augustine provided eloquent witnesses to this:

> He had power to lay down his life, and to take it again.... He by dying, straightway slew death in Himself; we, by His death are delivered from death.... He had no need of us, in order to work out our salvation; we, without him, can do nothing.... Lastly, although brethren die for brethren, yet no martyr's blood is ever shed for the remission of the sins of the brethren, as was the case in what he did for us. He did for us; and in this respect he bestowed on us aught for imitation, but for congratulation. In as far, then, as the martyrs have shed their blood for the brethren, so far have they exhibited such tokens of love as they themselves perceived at the table of the Lord. (*Tractate LXXXIV.2 on the Gospel of John 15:13*)[23]

The Christian Tradition asks that we recognize our sinfulness, and bring it to the table, that our sins might be forgiven: "This is my blood of the covenant, which is poured out for many for the forgiveness of sins" (Matt 26:28). Recognizing this perennial truth that lies at the heart of the Christian mystery, the renewed Liturgy of the Eucharist of the Roman Rite, restoring ancient traditions, opens with a public moment of silence when each participant reflects on her or his sinfulness and the community itself reflects on its sinfulness. As sinful individuals and as a sinful community, the Church then articulates its need for forgiveness by uttering one of its earliest prayers, often retaining the Greek expression *Kyrie eleison*: Lord, have mercy! Only then, once the need for forgiveness has been established, a prayer of reconciliation is prayed. The assembly responds, "Amen." The tone of the entire Liturgy of the Eucharist is set by this moment. Repentance is in place and forgiveness can be granted. The Eucharist, celebrating an assembly of repentant sinners who have been granted God's forgiveness, is underway.

> Our identity as Christians breaks out of the vicious circle of self-justifying judgment. It leaves behind the idolatrous forms of defensive, individualistic self-assertion, for the sake of a humble entry into the merciful universe of "*Our* Father." There grace reigns, Christ has died and risen for our sake, and all holiness comes from the Spirit.[24]

David Konstan has recently shown that the Old and the New Testaments, as well as the subsequent Church fathers, introduced a notion of forgiveness that was entirely unknown in Greek and Roman antiquity. This took place because of the introduction of the divine into what, to that point in reflection on human relationships, forgiveness was considered—an ethical concept. The biblical tradition, introducing God into the discourse, renders forgiveness theological: it has to do with the relationships between the human and the divine.[25] Anthony Kelly has rightly described forgiveness as part of "our identity as Christians." Faith in God and God's action of forgiveness for the fragile human condition through the death, resurrection, and ascension of Jesus makes forgiveness a cornerstone of Christian thought and practice. As John Chryssavgis notes,

> Christianity testifies that the past can be undone. It knows the mystery of obliterating, or rather renewing memory, of forgiveness and regeneration....One repents not because one is virtuous, but because human nature can change, because what is impossible for man is possible for God....Forgiveness, absolution is the culmination of repentance in response to sincerely felt compunction....It is a freely given grace of Christ and the Holy Spirit within the Church as the Body of Christ.[26]

God has made forgiveness possible by doing the impossible in the gift of his Son. The death, resurrection, and ascension of Jesus, as well as the gift of the Holy Spirit, are rendered present to the sinful believer in the "freely given grace of Christ and the Holy Spirit" at the celebration of the Eucharist. As such, a cornerstone of the Church's doctrine is articulated in the belief that the Eucharist is a celebration of forgiveness. The celebration of the Eucharist, source and summit of the Christian life (*LG* 10; *SC* 11), is an articulation of God's forgiveness, made available through the gift of his Son, Jesus Christ. If this were not the case, our "source and summit" could not claim to be part of our identity as Christians, and that flies in the face of two thousand years of Christian faith and practice. Articulating our Nicene-Constantinopolitan Creed, we believe in the doctrine of "the forgiveness of sins" and celebrate Eucharist accordingly.

A CONTEMPORARY DILEMMA

Catholics, led by a pope crying out for a renewed presence of radical mercy, insisting that "we are not living in an era of change but a change of era," face a critical dilemma. "Doctrine," not "mercy," determines Church law: believers who are in a permanent state of serious sin cannot approach the Table of the Lord and participate fully in it (*CJC* 915–16). Over the centuries, there have no doubt been many situations of enduring sinfulness where this law has been justifiably applied. Much of this sinfulness continues. I am aware that the argument of this study could lead to a conclusion that the only requirements for access to the eucharistic table are baptism, faith, and repentance. As we have seen, that was certainly the case in the first Christian millennium, when the Church catholic reflected on its mysteries. It has been practiced over recent decades by many Protestant communities. The contemporary ecumenical and theological debates surrounding grace and justification, Eucharist, ecclesiology, and ministry, to mention only a few, must continue. Without suggesting that all denominational boundaries might now be crossed, for the moment, as we conclude this study, it must be insisted that we are addressing a specifically Roman Catholic theological and disciplinary question. Much more can and must be said about ecumenical access to the eucharistic table before all Christians can join the celebration of Eucharist as forgiveness.[27]

Today, with the complexity of society, the changes in the way men and women relate to one another, the pressures of maintaining a social and professional life in an increasingly secular and anti-Christian world, to mention but some of the issues believing Christians must face, the situation of the divorced and remarried Catholic is crucial. There is hardly a Catholic family in the Western world that does not face this dilemma. Pope Francis has addressed this question honestly and realistically (*Amoris Laetitia* 298–99).[28] I have recently dealt with this question at some length in a study directed to all Christians, but especially to the leaders of the Roman Catholic community.[29] There is no need to revisit those reflections. A brief theological and pastoral note on Eucharist as the *communion* of the needy brings this study to a conclusion. I offer these brief closing thoughts, convinced that Pope Francis is exactly right: "Christian doctrine is not a closed system incapable of generating questions, doubts, interrogatives—but is alive, knows being unsettled, enlivened. It has a face that is not rigid, it has a body that moves and grows, it has soft flesh: it is called Jesus Christ."[30]

Our reflections on some New Testament evidence, and the development of eucharistic disciplines in the early Church, and among the fathers, indicated that there were good reasons for exclusion from the community, and thus from the Eucharist. However, it was clear that such exclusion was determined by practices that manifested erroneous beliefs, or the rejection of what God had done in and through Jesus Christ.[31] Both 1 Corinthians 5:1–8 and Hebrews 6:1–12 indicate that moral faults often arise from a faulty Christology (1 Cor 5:4–5, 7–8 and Heb 6:4–8) or a faulty ecclesiology (1 Cor 5). Similar results emerged from our analysis of a cross-section of early Christian writing. From the turn of the first and second centuries (*Didache*) until the later fathers of the Church (Maximus the Confessor), there is an awareness that baptism into the Christian "communion" was essential for participation in what we today call eucharistic "communion." Our approach to this central mystery of the Christian life must not be a "free-for-all."

The tradition of exclusion from the Eucharist of those who knowingly, willingly, consciously, and deliberately break "communion" with those who believe in Jesus as the Christ, the Son of God, and Savior must be maintained. Yet it is of equal concern that the Christian Church recognizes the truth of the New Testament's precious insight: the Eucharist is always a gift of the Lord to his failing community, a celebration of forgiveness. A balance must be maintained between an understanding of the Eucharist as a place where sinners gather to express repentance, to be nourished and challenged by their Lord, and a sacred encounter that must not be cheapened through the admission of those who have no right to such "communion" with its obligation of continual striving to live as Jesus lived. A prerequisite for such participation must be the recognition of sinfulness, repentance, and the willing acceptance of forgiveness. There can be no forgiveness where there is no recognition of guilt.

We have seen the importance of how the early Church understood

Jesus's presence to his failing disciples and their obligation to continue that "presence" in the celebration of the Eucharist. We are also aware that those who deliberately and publicly break "communion" (*koinōnia*) have no place at the celebration of our eucharistic "communion." There are good reasons to exclude from the eucharistic table those who arrogantly reject what God has done for us in and through the person of Jesus. Especially challenging in the contemporary Western world are the many cynical post-Catholics, who claim that they have "outgrown" the religion of their childish days and respond arrogantly to any attempt to give value to what God has done for us in Jesus Christ. They also tend to mock those who see the Catholic Church as a life-giving community. On "family occasions," or "to keep the parents happy," they feel free to participate fully in any eucharistic celebration, disregarding the outmoded ways of the Catholic Church when it is suggested that such actions are not coherent with their beliefs (or lack thereof). "Those who could not eat with Jesus were those who rejected him, not those whom he rejected: his welcome was for all who would respond to him. He made no exceptions."[32]

A discipline of exclusion, however, should not be applied to committed, baptized Catholics who come to the Eucharist, seeking forgiveness. We need to develop better criteria concerning admission to the Table of the Lord. Perhaps we could be guided by a better application of the double meaning of the word "communion" (*koinōnia*) used by Paul to great effect in 1 Corinthians 10:14–22. The "communion" created by genuinely eucharistic lives renders the "body of Christ" present in the Church's eucharistic celebrations. Those who recognize the imperfection and even the sinfulness of their lives, but have no other options, should not be excluded. One often finds a Christ-like gift of self in these situations. Many suffer deeply in the ambiguity of their situation, yet maintain their loyalty to the Christian Church and its values. Many find themselves in situations where life itself depends on a choice that excludes them from the Table of the Lord. In such situations a decision may not even be a choice, so much as a response forced on them by circumstances beyond their control. This can lead to the exclusion of those who commit themselves to a daily following of the crucified Christ. They are regularly found among the poor and suffering in society (see *Amoris Laetitia* 32–57, 291–300, 302–3). The only choices available to them are those that currently exclude them from the Lord's Table.[33]

Disciplines were linked to the sacrament of marriage in the period before its establishment among the seven sacraments (fifteenth to sixteenth centuries) that made sense in the society of that time. Lifelong marriage, although most likely a challenging way of life for many, especially for the women from poorer classes, was taken for granted. No doubt some men and women found that they could no longer continue as a couple, but such breakdowns are largely undocumented (except among the powerful), and there was no such institution as divorce (except for the powerful). We continue to apply those same disciplines as if the same sociosexual situation still existed, and as if Catholic practices were still the only Christian way of life available, as it was until the sixteenth century. Is this a very public case of what Pope Francis has called "a restoration of obsolete conduct and forms that no longer have the capacity of being significant culturally"?[34] Today's Church is called to show radical mercy in its ministry to a society where one marriage in three ends in divorce or permanent separation.[35] Outside these official figures, many persist in deeply damaging unhappy relationships or simply drift apart from one another into a form of unofficial separation and alternative unhappy liaisons. The impact of such relationships on children is well documented (see *Amoris Laetitia* 259–90 [the role of the family in educating children], 209 [the suffering of children in irregular marriages]). Current eucharistic practice generates an intolerable tension between faith and life for millions of Catholics.

Many who are in most need of "communion" with their eucharistic Lord and the eucharistic community that sings and prays together as they celebrate the presence of their forgiving Lord are simply denied that opportunity. An increasing number of pastors attempt to resolve such tension by adopting a practice called "internal forum." Good pastors, aware of the holiness of those who needlessly suffer from exclusion, decide to admit them to the Eucharist, leaving it to their own conscience, and request that they avoid all possible "scandal" in a community that may regard them as secretly "living in sin." This pastoral approach helps many, but it is unsatisfactory practice on two grounds. First, from a theological perspective, those concerned must live their "secret" in a way that damages an understanding of the Eucharist as a celebration of forgiveness. Could they not be directed to a full communion with the other "sinners" in the community who do not suffer from canonical penalties among whom they experience love and forgiveness? Second, admission to "communion" in this way damages the "communion," which is the celebrating Church. Some must "live their secret" in hidden silence. Pope Francis, unwilling to accept this widespread practice, suggests that it can lead to the impression that the Catholic Church adopts a "double standard" (*Amoris Laetitia* 300).[36]

In order to overcome this, Church leadership might take the bold step of establishing a process whereby divorced and remarried people would be admitted to full communion, despite their regrettable, but often unavoidable, situation in life. I am not qualified to indicate how the details of such a process might work. Its implementation would call for careful consultation with those involved, including Catholics in failed relationships seeking full communion, and subsequent legislation. As Pope Francis has pointed out, "Different communities will have to devise more practical and effective initiatives that respect both the Church's teaching and local problems and needs" (*Amoris Laetitia* 199). I suggest that the local ordinary, a pastor, and the community be involved in a formal recognition, and celebration, however simple, of a person (or a couple's) genuine quest for wholeness and holiness. This process may discern "that in a particular case no fault exists."[37] The Holy Father, without entering into detail, insists on the need to adopt "a process of accompaniment and discernment." He sets the agenda for this process: "For this discernment to happen, the following conditions must necessarily be present: humility, discretion and love for the Church and her teaching, a sincere search for God's will and a desire to make a more perfect response to it" (*Amoris Laetitia* 300). Such people yearn for the eucharistic celebration of forgiveness.

Currently, we are able to fly to the moon or from one side of the world to the other in 24 hours, communicate immediately with anyone in the world, cure illnesses that were once incurable, construct magnificent machines, build bridges crossing seas and valleys, buildings, cities, communities, and much more. But we cannot handle the sectarian violence and horrific brutality that surrounds us and erupts in our cities on a regular basis. We are supposed to be comforted by stern words from governments who promise that religious fundamentalism will be severely monitored by police and that an alliance of international military forces will wipe out the unacceptable cruel inhumanity of the jihadists. None of this will bear fruit; it will produce only more frustration and violence. Only from Pope Francis do we hear the words "mercy and forgiveness" in these death-dealing conflicts. We continue to spiral into widespread and vicious violence. There are many forms of violence, and some exist within the Christian Churches, as discrimination against women and the abuse of minors have eloquently shown. Can "mercy and forgiveness" show its face within the eucharistic discipline of the Church itself?

The pope is correct when he speaks of the need for the Catholic Church to face "a change of era." We have never been here before! Pope Francis leads the way when he challenges the Church, and through the witness of the Church, the whole world, with his message of mercy and forgiveness. But the message must first be listened to by the Christian Churches, especially Francis's own Catholic Church, and put into practice so that it can be a prophetic appeal to all societies. It is proving to be difficult, even for a Church that can no longer hold its head high as an untainted moral authority.[38] As the saying goes, "The truth hurts." This is especially so when we hide behind a carefully constructed, age-old self-image. The hard-hearted rejection of others makes us spiritually ugly. Being found out is therefore humbling. In a world of God-given mercy and forgiveness, the whole truth is a source of healing and hope, and it offers new life. Paul says it well: "I will boast all the more gladly of my weaknesses, so that the power of Christ may dwell in me" (2 Cor 12:9).

CONCLUSION

Perhaps the present challenging times, when even some of Christianity's most beautiful and significant contributions are being attacked by an aggressive secularism, are a grace, a challenging gift of God. Is this a God-given time to accept the fundamental truth about mercy and forgiveness: they have their origins in God? As Pope Francis puts it,

> We have known a love that is prior to any of our own efforts, a love that constantly opens doors and encourages. If we accept that God's love is unconditional, that the Father's love cannot be bought or sold, then we will become capable of showing boundless love and forgiving others even when they have wronged us. (*Amoris Laetitia* 108)

Despite rigid authoritarianism and an apparent inability to admit sinfulness on the part of some Catholic leaders, is it beyond the capacity of the Catholic Church to institute a process that would be administered locally, under the general supervision of the local ordinary, to dispense eucharistic mercy and forgiveness to those it has traditionally excluded from the Lord's Table? Can Catholics joyfully and gratefully accept the holiness of fellow Christians, recognizing their ambiguity and their search for the loving presence of the crucified and risen Christ, no matter what their situation might be? My now long Catholic experience teaches me that we can, although not without difficulty.[39] The opposition that Pope Francis is meeting from certain sections of the Catholic Church, especially in the United States, indicates that "forgiveness" of those whose marriages have failed is not part of what they accept as Catholic doctrine. He recognizes and respects those views (see *Amoris Laetitia* 308) but begs to differ: "Jesus wants a Church attentive to the goodness which the Holy Spirit sows in the midst of human weakness."

The above suggested process would recognize that sin has occurred, as it does with all of us. It would equally recognize the presence of sorrow, pain, and repentance, lived in a relationship of faithful love and fruitfulness. This is something that all people who participate in the Eucharist should embrace, not only those who are "institutionally" excluded from "the communion." "Let anyone among you who is without sin be the first to throw a stone at her" (John 8:7). All four Gospels record that the original disciples recognized this need. As is well known, and as this study has further analyzed, baptism, repentance for sins, and God's forgiveness have always provided the building blocks for Christian life. As John Chryssavgis puts it, "Man in his sinfulness is loved by God if he can just keep moving towards God. When one *does* fall, if one only cries out with confidence, the fall is not into nothingness but into the arms of God stretched open once and for all on the Cross."[40]

Recognizing their sinfulness, the baptized turn confidently to the presence of a loving and forgiving God in the celebration of the crucified and risen Christ at the Eucharist. It has always been a celebration of forgiveness for all whose repentance, hope, and love, enlivened by the Holy Spirit, lead them to seek communion with God, Jesus Christ, and one another.

NOTES

PREFACE

1. For a reliable Greek text and English translation of the Apostolic Fathers (*Didache*, Ignatius of Antioch), see Michael W. Holmes, *The Apostolic Fathers: Greek Texts and English Translations*, 3rd ed. (Grand Rapids, MI: Baker Academic, 2007). For Justin Martyr, see Leslie William Barnard, *St. Justin Martyr the First and Second Apologies*, Ancient Christian Writers 56 (New York: Paulist Press, 1997).

2. Holmes, *Apostolic Fathers*, 359.

3. The formal structure of the eucharistic liturgy did not begin to appear until the fifth century, in liturgies associated with Gregory (335–94) and Basil (330–79). For more detail, see below, chap. 1, n. 3.

4. Congregation for Divine Worship and the Discipline of the Sacraments, *Liturgiam Authenticam: On the Use of Vernacular Languages in the Publication of the Books of the Roman Liturgy* (Vatican City: Editrice Libreria Vaticana, 2001).

5. The difficulties encountered since the promulgation of *Sacrosanctum Concilium* stem from the Council fathers' decision to authorize Episcopal Conferences to oversee such adaptation (*SC* 40) and the subsequent direction taken by the Congregation for Divine Worship to assume all such responsibility, as indicated by *Liturgiam Authenticam*.

6. See the synthesis of Adalbert Hamman and Mario Maritano, "Eucharist," in *Encyclopedia of Ancient Christianity Produced by the Institutum Patristicum Augustinianum* (Downers Grove, IL: IVP Academic, 2014), 1:854–57.

7. Holmes, *Apostolic Fathers*, 359.

8. Barnard, *St. Justin Martyr*, 70.

9. On this question, see Francis J. Moloney, *A Body Broken for a Broken People: Divorce, Remarriage, and the Eucharist* (New York: Paulist Press, 2016), 13–39.

10. Pope Francis, Post-Synodal Apostolic Exhortation *Amoris Laetitia* (Vatican City: Editrice Vaticana, 2016). Many striking passages could be cited, but the pope's sentiments can be heard in his words: "No one can be condemned for ever, because that is not the logic of the Gospel!" (no. 297).

11. Pope Francis, *Amoris Laetitia*, 301–3, turns to Thomas Aquinas's teaching on "ignorance," suggesting that many contemporary Catholics are not "conscious of grave sin."

12. *Catechism of the Catholic Church* (Homebush: St Pauls Publications, 1997), 356.

13. Anthony J. Kelly and Francis J. Moloney, *The Experience of God in the Johannine Writings* (Mahwah, NJ: Paulist Press, 2003).

CHAPTER 1

1. The use of biblical texts to address later religious and theological issues and situations is legitimate, and necessary. However, it is damaging to "accommodate" a text in a way that totally neglects the original context and meaning.

2. For a more detailed study of 1 Cor 11:17–34, much of which is resumed here, see Moloney, *A Body Broken*, 41–69.

3. A historical note is called for. Surprising as it may seem, the formal structure of the eucharistic liturgy did not begin to appear until the fifth century, in liturgies associated with Gregory (335–94) and Basil (330–79). There is no historically verifiable line of development prior to that time. See Robert J. Daly, "From the New Testament to the Liturgies of the Gospel Age," *Theological Studies* 68 (2007): 3–22. Perhaps equally surprising, there is no evidence of the use of the words of institution in liturgies prior to the fourth century. See Robert F. Taft, "Mass without the Consecration? The Historical Agreement on the Eucharist between the Catholic Church and the Assyrian Churches of the East, Promulgated 26 October 2001," *Worship* 77 (2003): 482–509.

4. In his deeply flawed recent book, Brad Pitre, *Jesus and the Last Supper* (Grand Rapids: Eerdmans, 2015), confidently claims that he has uncovered who Jesus thought he was, what he said and did at the last supper, and what it meant for him and for the disciples. If he is correct, of course, his reading of the Last Supper would be our earliest witness. Among many serious critical issues, he devotes little or no

attention to the impact of the theological and pastoral contribution of the inspired evangelists on the Gospel narratives. The gospel accounts are not "history" in the way Pitre reconstructs it (although there is a great deal of history there), but a proclamation of what God has done in and through Jesus. Pitre's understanding of the significance of the Last Supper is rich, but attributing it all to the person of Jesus of Nazareth is unconvincing. It requires a remarkable Christology of Jesus of Nazareth.

5. For an outstanding study of Paul's use of the memory of the earliest Church in establishing the significance of Jesus's self-gift in death, see Dale C. Allison Jr., *Constructing Jesus. Memory, Imagination, and History* (Grand Rapids: Baker Academic, 2010), 392–433.

6. See the important comment of Joseph Ratzinger, "Sacred Scripture in the Life of the Church," in *Commentary on the Documents of Vatican II*, ed. Herbert Vorgrimler, 3 vols. (London: Burns & Oates/ Herder & Herder, 1969), 3:268: "A reference to the ecclesial nature of exegesis on the one hand, and to its methodological correctness on the other (*DV* 12), again expresses the inner tension of Church exegesis, which can no longer be removed, but must be simply accepted as tension." See further, Francis J. Moloney, *Reading the New Testament in the Church: A Primer for Pastors, Religious Educators, and Believers* (Grand Rapids, MI: Baker Academic, 2015), 191–201.

7. See especially John Fotopoulos, *Food Offered to Idols in Roman Corinth: A Social-Rhetorical Reconsideration of 1 Corinthians 8:1—11:1*, Wissenschaftliche Untersuchungen zum Neuen Testament 2.151 (Tübingen: Mohr Siebeck, 2003). Fotopoulos provides an excellent survey of scholarship, and the religious and cultural settings of Roman Corinth that impacted on the Corinthian Christians, pp. 1–48 (research) and 49–178 (religious and cultural settings).

8. Benjamin A. Edsall, *Paul's Witness to Formative Early Christian Instruction*, Wissenschaftliche Untersuchungen zum Neuen Testament 2.365 (Tübingen: Mohr Siebeck, 2014), 98–121, 170–75, shows this convincingly by analyzing Paul's relentless discussion of troublesome issues in 1 Corinthians, and the indications of multiple interventions in 2 Corinthians (see the summary in Edsall, *Paul's Witness*, 59).

9. See Brendan J. Byrne, *Reckoning with Romans: A Contemporary Reading of Paul's Gospel*, Good News Studies 18 (Wilmington, DE: Michael Glazier, 1986), 20–25; Moloney, *Reading the New Testament in the Church*, 93–106.

10. For a helpful study of this crucial passage, see Brendan Byrne, *Paul and the Christian Woman* (Homebush: St Pauls Publications, 1988), 1–14.

11. Paul's discussion of the roles of women in the assemblies has generated a great deal of debate. Some have even suggested that 1 Corinthians 11:2–16 is so out of character that it must be a later insertion. The proposal is widely rejected. For discussions of this difficult passage, see Byrne, *Paul and the Christian Woman*, 31–58; and Pheme Perkins, *First Corinthians*, Paideia Commentaries on the New Testament (Grand Rapids: Baker Academic, 2012), 132–41. See also the exhaustive treatments of Joseph A. Fitzmyer, *First Corinthians*, The Anchor Yale Bible 32 (New Haven: Yale University Press, 2008), 404–25; and Raymond F. Collins, *First Corinthians*, Sacra Pagina 7 (Collegeville, MN: Liturgical Press, 1999), 393–424. Collins aptly titles this section of his commentary, "Let Men Be Men and Women Be Women."

12. For a clear presentation of the divided community, see Jerome Murphy-O'Connor, "Eucharist and Community in First Corinthians," *Worship* 50 (1976): 370–72 and 51 (1977): 64–69.

13. Care is called for, as Paul does not advocate a "free for all" admission to the table. The expulsion from the community of the man involved in an incestuous relationship in 1 Corinthians 5:1–6 that we will consider in chapter 3 indicates this fact.

14. The interplay between the "communion" of a group of believing Christians and the use of the expression "communion" to speak of full participation in the eucharistic celebration by receiving the bread and wine will be an important consideration later in this study. See below, pp. 94–97.

15. For a study of the meaning of *koinōnia* here, see Xavier Léon-Dufour, *Sharing the Eucharistic Bread: The Witness of the New Testament*, trans. Matthew J. O'Connell (New York: Paulist Press, 1997), 209–11. The term *metechein* is used by Paul as an equivalent to *koinōnein*.

16. Jerome Murphy-O'Connor, *1 Corinthians*, New Testament Message 10 (Wilmington, DE: Michael Glazier, 1979), 97. See also Léon-Dufour, *Sharing the Eucharistic Bread*, 211–13.

17. Günther Bornkamm, "Lord's Supper and Church in Paul," in *Early Christian Experience* (London: SCM Press, 1969), 127.

18. On the importance of vv. 1–13 for the whole argument of chapter 10, see Fotopoulos, *Food Offered to Idols*, 208–23.

19. It is helpful to notice that Paul uses this same "reminding" technique on two other occasions in 1 Corinthians. In 11:23, he recalls what they had learned from him about the Eucharist, and in 15:1–3a, what they had learned from him about the resurrection. On both of these occasions Paul also indicates that what they had learned from him was an earlier Tradition he had received.

20. Gerd Theissen, "Social Integration and Sacramental Activity: An Analysis of 1 Cor 11:17–34," in *The Social Setting of Pauline Christianity: Essays on Corinth* (Philadelphia: Fortress, 1982), 165–66.

21. On this internal logic of 11:17–34, see Fitzmyer, *First Corinthians*, 426.

22. Luc Dequeker and Willem Zuidema, "The Eucharist and St Paul: 1 Cor. 11.17–34," *Concilium* 4 (1968): 28.

23. C. Kingsley Barrett, *The First Epistle to the Corinthians*, Black's New Testament Commentaries (London: A. & C. Black, 1971), 263–64.

24. For an excellent detailed discussion of the history and meaning of the Pauline version of the institution narrative, see Fitzmyer, *First Corinthians*, 436–44.

25. See Francis J. Moloney, "Synchronic Interpretation," in *The Oxford Encyclopedia of Biblical Interpretation*, ed. Steven McKenzie, 2 vols. (Oxford/New York: Oxford University Press, 2013), 2:345–54.

26. This is particularly powerful if the textually disturbed v. 24 is to be read as "my body, broken for you." In defense of this reading, see Collins, *First Corinthians*, 432.

27. See Peter Henrici, "'Do this in remembrance of me': The sacrifice of Christ and the sacrifice of the faithful," *Communio: International Catholic Review* 12 (1985): 146–57; and Fitzmyer, *First Corinthians*, 440–41.

28. Henrici, "Do this in remembrance of me," 148–49.

29. See Beverley Gaventa, "'You Proclaim the Lord's Death': 1 Corinthians 11:26 and Paul's Understanding of Worship," *Review and Expositor* 80 (1983): 377–87.

30. See Jerome Kodell, *The Eucharist in the New Testament*, Zacchaeus Studies New Testament (Wilmington, DE: Michael Glazier, 1989), 80: "Scholars have become aware that both ideas may be contained in the call to remember: the Eucharist as a reminder to God and as a reminder to the followers of Jesus. God is reminded of his covenant promises in Jesus so that he will fulfil them, and the disciples are

reminded of Jesus' self-gift in life and death so that they may imitate his example."

31. Henrici, "Do this in remembrance of me," 155.

32. Nils A. Dahl, "Anamnesis: Memory and Commemoration in Early Christianity," in *Jesus in the Memory of the Early Church* (Minneapolis: Augsburg, 1976), 13. See also pp. 21–24 on eucharistic memory, concluding, "Early Christianity was not only faith and worship, but also a way of life" (24).

33. See, for example, Antonio Piolanti, *The Holy Eucharist* (New York: Desclée, 1961), 45–46. But the Catholic scholar, Murphy-O'Connor, *1 Corinthians*, 114, comments as follows: "It is sometimes said that what Paul demands here is that participants distinguish the eucharist from common food, but this does not fit the context, and betrays a preoccupation with the doctrine of the real presence characteristic of a much later era."

34. See Barrett, *The First Epistle to the Corinthians*, 273–75; Bornkamm, "Lord's Supper and Church in Paul," 148–52.

35. See Fitzmyer, *First Corinthians*, 446–47.

36. Ibid., 446.

37. First Corinthians 11:30 speaks of the weak, the sick, and the dead in the community, and it links this phenomenon to their poor use of the Lord's Table. This difficult verse indicates that the destructive powers of old age, sickness, and death are still active, but it also means that they are sent to them from the Lord to execute his judgment. See Collins, *First Corinthians*, 436–37. Fitzmyer, *First Corinthians*, 448, comments, "Afflictions such as sickness and death may reveal to us the Lord's judgment, but they really have a medicinal and educative purpose, that we may not share in the long run in any eschatological judgment."

38. Léon-Dufour, *Sharing the Eucharistic Bread*, 229.

39. Hans Conzelmann, *1 Corinthians: A Commentary on the First Epistle to the Corinthians*, trans. James W. Leitch, Hermeneia (Philadelphia: Fortress, 1975), 201. See also Collins, *First Corinthians*, 435–41.

40. Theissen, "Social Integration and Sacramental Activity," 168.

CHAPTER 2

1. The names Mark, Matthew, Luke, and John were added to the four gospel accounts late in the second century in order to preserve the

uniqueness of each account. At that time, there was a tendency to generate a "compilation" of all four. The most famous attempt was the now-lost *Diatesseron* by Tatian (c. 120–80 CE). Out of respect for the tradition, I will use these names to refer to the four evangelists, even though we do not know with any certainty the identity of the historical authors.

2. Luke's reference to a second generation who "set down" orderly accounts indicates that there were earlier written documents. One was Mark's Gospel, and perhaps others that we no longer have. Scholars claim Gospel material found in Matthew and Luke but not in Mark (mainly Jesus's teaching) probably comes from such an early written "source." They name this document (which we do not have) "Q," the first letter of the German word *Quelle* ("source"). On this, see the very clear introduction by John S. Kloppenborg, *Q, The Earliest Gospels: An Introduction to the Original Stories and Sayings of Jesus* (Louisville, KY: Westminster John Knox, 2008), 1–40.

3. The expression was famously coined by J. Louis Martyn, *History and Theology in the Fourth Gospel*, The New Testament Library, 3rd ed. (Louisville, KY: Westminster John Knox, 2003).

4. A number of contemporary scholars reject this process. I fail to understand why. Anyone telling a story of the past to a present audience (e.g., parents telling fairy tales or family history to their children) *necessarily* generates a "two-level drama," mediating a message from the past to address the present situation.

5. For such a study, much of which is summarized below, see Moloney, *A Body Broken*, 71–203.

6. For more detailed discussion of Matthew 14:13–21 and 15:32–39, see Moloney, *A Body Broken*, 107–15. See especially p. 125n26.

7. The earliest use of *ta klasmata* to speak of the bread of the Eucharist is found in the *Didache* 9:4. Another early reference is found in *1 Clement* 34:7.

8. Commentators note that Matthew 14:13–21 omits the references to the shepherd and also to the gathering of the people into groups of fifty and one hundred. But the setting is clearly in Israel.

9. For more detail, see Francis J. Moloney, *The Gospel of Mark: A Commentary* (Grand Rapids, MI: Baker Academic, 2012), 152–56.

10. For studies of these passages, see Moloney, *A Body Broken*, 130–35 (Luke 9:1–10), and 168–73 (John 6:1–15).

11. Matthew often marks the beginning and end of a literary section of his account with summary statements of what is about to happen or what has concluded. This is especially clear in 26:1–2, a passion predication not found in the other Gospels. It is the only such prediction where no mention is made of the resurrection.

12. The practice of "framing" episodes (called "intercalation") is common in Mark's Gospel. The most famous "frames" are the encounter with Jairus, the healing of the woman with the flow of blood, the raising of Jairus's daughter (5:21–43), Jesus's cursing of the fig tree, the ending of cult in the Jerusalem Temple, and the discovery of the dead fig tree the following day (11:12–25). For a good study of this Markan characteristic (followed here by Matthew), see Tom Shepherd, "The Narrative Function of Markan Intercalation," *New Testament Studies* 41 (1995): 522–40.

13. Léon-Dufour, *Sharing the Eucharistic Bread*, 60–62, 117–18, 130–32, 195–96, rightly insists on this "dialogic" character of the Markan/Matthean account.

14. See ibid., 148; William D. Davies and Dale C. Allison Jr., *A Critical and Exegetical Commentary on the Gospel of Matthew*, International Critical Commentary, 3 vols. (Edinburgh: T. & T. Clark, 1988–97), 3:474–75.

15. For an outstanding survey, see Sherri Brown, *Gift upon Gift: Covenant through Word in the Gospel of John*, Princeton Theological Monograph Series 144 (Eugene, OR: Pickwick Publications, 2010), 23–67. On covenant in the prophets, see pp. 54–62.

16. Ibid., 61.

17. Ulrich Luz, *Matthew*, trans. James E. Crowe, Hermeneia, 3 vols. (Minneapolis: Fortress, 2001–7), 3:381–82.

18. Jerome Neyrey, *The Passion according to Luke: A Redaction Study of Luke's Soteriology* (New York: Paulist Press, 1985), 10.

19. Robert J. Karris, *Luke: Artist and Theologian: Luke's Passion Account as Literature* (New York: Paulist Press, 1985), 70, whimsically remarks, "Jesus got himself crucified because of the way he ate."

20. Léon-Dufour, *Sharing the Eucharistic Bread*, 233.

21. See Moloney, *A Body Broken*, 138–39.

22. Among others, see Luke T. Johnson, *The Gospel of Luke*, Sacra Pagina 3 (Collegeville, MN: Liturgical Press, 1991), 336–50. Johnson is especially helpful on the "farewell discourse" genre on pp. 347–49.

23. See Robert C. Tannehill, *The Narrative Unity of Luke-Acts: A Literary Interpretation*, 2 vols. (Philadelphia: Fortress, 1986), 263: "Whether or not 22:14–38 technically belongs to a recognized genre which can be called 'farewell discourse' or 'farewell address,' Jesus' words are uttered in the light of his impending death and with awareness of the new situation which the apostles are entering, as appears in the command to 'do this for my memory,' the effort to prepare the apostles for their new role as leaders in 22:24–27, and a gift of a share in Jesus' royal power in 22:28–30." See his fine commentary of 22:14–38 on pp. 263–70.

24. Paul S. Minear, "Some Glimpses of Luke's Sacramental Theology," *Worship* 44 (1970): 326. I am following majority scholarly tradition, accepting that vv. 19b–20, not found in some early manuscripts, are original.

25. For what follows, I am depending on the scheme of Neyrey, *The Passion according to Luke*, 6–8. Although scholars have long been aware of the literary form of a farewell speech, the uncovering of a large number of "testaments" at Qumran has led to increased interest from Christian scholars. Originally pre-Christian, the present text of these testaments has numerous Christian interpolations, but they offer evidence of the early Christian use of a Hebrew scriptural tradition.

26. For an introduction and an annotated critical text of this document (prepared by Howard C. Kee), see James H. Charlesworth, ed., *The Old Testament Pseudepigrapha*, 2 vols. (London: Darton, Longman & Todd, 1983), 1:775–828. Originally pre-Christian, the *Testaments of the Twelve Patriarchs* have numerous Christian interpolations, but they offer evidence of the early Christian use of a Hebrew scriptural tradition.

27. Neyrey, *The Passion according to Luke*, 31–37, shows that Jesus's words are a commissioning of Peter, suggesting that v. 32b is comparable to the commissioning of Peter found in Matt 16:17–18 and John 21:15–17.

28. Kodell, *The Eucharist in the New Testament*, 117.

29. For a more detailed study of John 13:1–38, see Francis J. Moloney, *Love in the Gospel of John: An Exegetical, Theological, and Literary Study* (Grand Rapids, MI: Baker Academic, 2013), 99–117.

30. See the excellent note on John's use of the double "amen" in John H. Bernard, *A Critical and Exegetical Commentary on the Gospel of*

John, International Critical Commentary, 2 vols. (Edinburgh: T. & T. Clark, 1928), 1:66–67.

31. Most commentators read 13:1–30 as a unit and see vv. 31–38 as the beginning of the discourse that follows from 14:1—16:33. For the above case, see Francis J. Moloney, "The Literary Unity of John 13,1–38," *Ephemerides Theologicae Lovanienses* 91 (2015): 33–53.

32. The Greek phrase demands this meaning. See C. Kingsley Barrett, *The Gospel according to St. John*, 2nd ed. (London: SPCK, 1978), 439.

33. The link with baptism is made through the Greek expression *echein meros met'emou* ("to have part with me"). As Barrett, *St. John*, 441, explains, "John has penetrated beneath the surface of baptism as an ecclesiastical rite, seen it in its relation to the Lord's death, into which converts were baptized (cf. Rom. 6.3), and thus integrated it into the humble act of love in which the Lord's death was set forth before the passion." Barrett describes Peter as in danger of having "no share in the benefits of Jesus' passion, and no place among his people."

34. R. Alan Culpepper, "The Johannine *Hypodeigma*: A Reading of John 13:1–38," *Semeia* 53 (1991): 144.

35. The English captures this balance, but the original Greek is very clear: *ei TAUTA oidate* (conditional)—*makarioi este* (beatitude)—*ean poiēte AUTA* (conditional).

36. The use of "I am he" in the Gospel of John is based in the revelation of the name of God to Moses as "I am who I am" in Exodus 3:14. The precise expression "I am he" was used throughout the Old Testament to refer to the revealing presence of God (see Deut 32:39; Exod 41:4; 43:10–11, 25; 46:4; 48:12; Isa 43:10; 45:18). John takes this tradition further by having Jesus boldly proclaim, "I am he" (see 4:26; 6:20; 8:24, 28, 58; 18:5–8), and thus claim that he is the revealer of God par excellence.

37. Strangely, the 28th edition of the *Novum Testamentum Graece* places the Greek of "he took and" in brackets in the Greek text (*lambanei kai*), but the NRSV does not even mention it as a possibility in its textual notes. See Nestle-Aland, *Novum Testamentum Graece. Greek-English New Testament* (Stuttgart: Deutsche Bibelgesellschaft, 2013), 349.

38. Augustine, *In Johannis Evangelium Tractatus* CXXIV, LXII.1–6. Augustine damns Judas on the evidence of 1 Corinthians 11:29 and Luke 22, but he nevertheless states that he has been gifted by God's

grace. Augustine's Latin original is memorable: "Quid erat autem panis traditori datus, nisi demonstratio cui gratiae fuisset ingratus."

39. This principle of interpretation, in my opinion, renders vain all attempts at historical reconstructions. The voice of the Gospel is lost in unreachable historical reconstruction. Most recently, see Pitre, *Jesus and the Last Supper*.

40. For a more detailed study of Luke 24:13–35, on which the following is based, see Francis J. Moloney, *The Resurrection of the Messiah: A Narrative Commentary of the Resurrection Accounts in the Four Gospels* (New York: Paulist Press, 2013), 81–86.

41. For a eucharistic reading of Luke 24:36–46, a close parallel with vv. 13–35, see Moloney, *A Body Broken*, 150–52.

CHAPTER 3

1. It is sometimes suggested that the passage from Matthew's Sermon on the Mount about being reconciled to one's brother or sister before leaving a gift before the altar (Matt 5:23–24) is pertinent to this discussion. It does not appear, however, that these words of Jesus are associated with the early practice of Eucharist. Many claim that they go back to Jesus himself, and that they presuppose the sacrificial system in Jerusalem. See the discussion in Davies and Allison, *Matthew*, 1:516–18; Luz, *Matthew*, 1:240.

2. The social situation of the communities of the early Church would have led any decision to exclude a person from the community to impact immediately on her or his access to the Lord's Table.

3. Jewish celebrations of God's saving intervention into Israel's history were "remembered" on the Sabbath, Pentecost, Passover, Tabernacles, and other feasts. These "memories" (*zikkarōn*) were not simply recalling of times past, but "remembering" in ritual and words that rendered the God of the Sabbath, Pentecost, Passover, Tabernacles, and so on *present to the celebrating community*. This is explicit in the words of Jesus, found in Paul and Luke: "Do this in remembrance [Greek: *anamnēsis*] of me" (1 Cor 11:24, 25; Luke 22:19). See the important study of Fritz Chenderlin, *"Do This as my Memorial": The Semantic and Conceptual Background and Value of* Anamnēsis *in 1 Corinthians 11:24–25*, Analecta Biblica 99 (Rome: Biblical Institute Press, 1982), especially pp. 88–127.

4. Conzelmann, *1 Corinthians*, 96. Among the Roman authors, it is discussed by Tacitus, Apuleius, Gaius, Cicero, Catullus, and Martial.

5. Perkins, *First Corinthians*, 91–92, suggests that the community is not moving against this person because he belongs to the Corinthian elite. This is the source of the "arrogance," a sense of superiority.

6. A number of interesting questions surround v. 3, as well as the theological or psychological meaning of "in spirit." Paul takes it for granted that he has the authority to speak to them in this fashion, even in his absence. As both letters to Corinth indicate, there were some in Corinth who questioned this. Paul tells little of Jesus's life and teaching, but it is the authority of Jesus ("in the name of") that he exercises.

7. For a careful study of the Old Testament antecedents, expulsion from Qumran, and Rabbinic Judaism, see Göran Forkman, *The Limits of Religious Community: Expulsion from the Religious Community within the Qumran Sect, within Rabbinic Judaism, and within Primitive Christianity*, trans. Pearl Sjölander, Coniectanea Biblica New Testament Series 5 (Lund: Gleerup, 1972), 16–114.

8. Barrett, *First Epistle*, 126.

9. Ibid., 127. Among others, Collins, *First Corinthians*, 213, claims that Paul is not writing about the man's "spirit," but about the "spirit" that is the community. Thus, the man is condemned without hope so that the community, "his spirit," may be saved. This is an unlikely suggestion as the spirit is identified as "his." See the discussion, coming to this conclusion, in Perkins, *First Corinthians*, 92–93.

10. Fitzmyer, *First Corinthians*, 240–41, objects that the Greek word used (*zymē*) does not mean "yeast," but "old, sour dough that had been subjected to fermenting juices and stored away (see Luke 13:21) until it was used in new dough as a rising agent, to make the new bread light and palatable." This is attractive, especially in the light of the "old" in vv. 6–8.

11. Barrett, *First Epistle*, 128.

12. It is sometimes attractively suggested that Paul was writing to the Corinthians from Ephesus at Passover time in 54 CE. This makes his appeal to Passover practices (the yeast) and the Christian Passover (the paschal lamb) especially effective. See Collins, *First Corinthians*, 208.

13. Murphy-O'Connor, *1 Corinthians*, 43.

14. See Fitzmyer, *First Corinthians*, 229–30, 236–37.

15. Forkman, *The Limits of Religious Community*, 149. More generally on the theological motivation for a Pauline understanding of exclusion "soon, but not yet," see pp. 191–93. Citation on p. 193.

16. The document also bears some characteristics of a letter, especially in the instructions of its ending (13:1–25). Raymond E. Brown, *An Introduction to the New Testament*, Anchor Bible Reference Library (New York: Doubleday, 1997), 690, helpfully suggests, "Perhaps we should settle for a relatively simple description of Hebrews as a written sermon or homily with an epistolary ending."

17. For an overview of the literary structure and theology of Hebrews, see Moloney, *Reading the New Testament in the Church*, 174–79.

18. See the good discussion of this question in Craig R. Koester, *Hebrews*, The Anchor Bible 36 (New York: Doubleday, 2001), 312–13. Koester points to the use of *adunaton* in the proximate 6:12 that states it is impossible for God to lie. This does not mean that he *could not* lie, as he can do everything. But God does not lie!

19. In v. 4, the author refers to those who have "tasted the heavenly gift." Some commentators see this as a reference to Eucharist, but it lacks the detail required for such a link. It indicates a participation in the life of grace. See, among others, Harold W. Attridge, *The Epistle to the Hebrews,* Hermeneia (Philadelphia: Fortress, 1989), 170; Koester, *Hebrews*, 314.

20. Koester, *Hebrews*, 321. This rhetoric is recognized by all major commentators. See, for example, Attridge, *Hebrews*, 167; William L. Lane, *Hebrews*, Word Biblical Commentary 47, 2 vols. (Nashville: Thomas Nelson, 1991), 1:145–46; Luke Timothy Johnson, *Hebrews: A Commentary*, The New Testament Library (Louisville, KT: Westminster John Knox, 2006), 161: "hypothetical apostasy." See especially James W. Thompson, *Hebrews*, Paideia Commentaries on the New Testament (Grand Rapids: Baker Academic, 2008), 135. He concludes, "Since this apostasy has not occurred, the author's words remain hypothetical. His words are intended to shock readers into recognizing the cost of abandoning God's heavenly gift."

21. For this suggestion, see Attridge, *Hebrews*, 171–72.

22. The NRSV renders the Greek *anastaurountas* as "crucify again." But the prefix *ana* does not indicate "again." It stresses the act of "lifting up." See, Koester, *Hebrews*, 315.

23. Brooke F. Westcott, *The Epistle to the Hebrews: The Greek Text with Notes and Essays* (London: Macmillan, 1889), 151.

24. Forkman, *The Limits of Religious Community*, 176–77, regards Heb 6:4–8 and 10:26–31 that deals with those who "wilfully persist in sin after having received the knowledge of the truth," as not referring to expulsion, "but rather to a general exhortation to watchfulness" (p. 177).

25. For a more detailed and lucid study of patristic witnesses to eucharistic thought and practice, see Paul F. Bradshaw and Maxwell Johnson, *The Eucharistic Liturgies: Their Evolution and Interpretation*, Alcuin Club Collections 87 (London: SPCK, 2012), 1–136. For an ambitious lively evaluation of the period, see Diarmaid MacCulloch, *A History of Christianity: The First Three Thousand Years* (London: Allen Lane, 2009), 19–228.

26. See the summary of the discussion in Holmes, *The Apostolic Fathers*, 337–39. Kurt Niederwimmer, *The Didache: A Commentary*, trans. Linda M. Maloney, Hermeneia (Minneapolis: Fortress, 1998), 52–55, suggests that the traditions that formed the *Didache* come from the first century, and the document probably appeared between 110–20 CE.

27. For more detail, see Bradshaw and Johnson, *Eucharistic Liturgies*, 14–19.

28. See the discussion in Niederwimmer, *The Didache*, 153.

29. Some have suggested that only the community meal is intended by "do not give what is holy," but is most probably the sacramental celebration of the Lord's Supper. See Niederwimmer, *The Didache*, 153–54.

30. For a full-scale commentary on the letters of Ignatius, see William R. Schoedel, *Ignatius of Antioch: A Commentary on the Letters of Ignatius of Antioch*, Hermeneia (Philadelphia: Fortress, 1985). See also the concise introduction to Ignatius and his letters in Holmes, *The Apostolic Fathers*, 166–81.

31. See Schoedel, *Ignatius of Antioch*, 21. Schoedel comments on Ignatius's insistence on the link between the Eucharist and unity: "The link is made all the clearer by the association of the sacred meal with the image of the altar which in Ignatius is not used to indicate the sacrificial character of the meal but to symbolize solidarity (*Eph.* 5.2;

Mag. 7.2; Tr. 7.2; *Phd.* 4). And it is this solidarity that is signified by the presence of the Lord at or in the sacred meal."

32. For speculation on the reasons for Ignatius's insistence on the authority of the bishop and the presbyters, see Schoedel, *Ignatius of Antioch*, 12–14; Holmes, *Apostolic Fathers*, 166–68. Ignatius is the earliest written witness to this tradition that became so important in later Christianity.

33. See the extensive commentary of Schoedel, *Ignatius of Antioch*, 235–42. Schoedel identifies the opponents as "docetists," people who do not accept the fully human condition of Jesus Christ. He also insists that they are seeking ecclesiastical privilege (pp. 235–36). This undermines the Eucharist and the saving effects of resurrection.

34. Ignatius points out that these people "ignorantly deny him," but their crisis is created by the fact that they "rather have been denied by him, for they are advocates of death rather than of the truth" (*Smyrneans* 5:1). This sentiment recalls Heb 6:4–8.

35. Schoedel, *Ignatius of Antioch*, 240. On the crucial role of mutual love of early Christianity, see the study of Rodney Stark, *The Rise of Christianity* (Princeton: Princeton University Press, 1996).

36. See Bradshaw and Johnson, *Eucharistic Liturgies*, 26–30.

37. The word used in the translation reflects the awkward choice of Justin to make a verb of the noun *Eucharist*. It is found in other early Christian authors. It conveys the meaning but is very difficult to render in English.

38. See Andrew B. McGowan, "The Meals of Jesus and the Meals of the Church: Eucharistic Origins and the Admission to Communion," in *Studia Liturgica Diversa: Essays in Honor of Paul F. Bradshaw*, ed. Maxwell E. Johnson and L. Edward Phillips (Portland, OR: Pastoral Press, 2004), 101–15.

39. His views fed into the later heresy of Donatism (after Donatus, bishop of Carthage). Subsequent to the persecution of Diocletian in 303–4, Christians who had lapsed were rebaptized by Donatus, and his breakaway hard-line Church in North Africa. Donatism took hold in North Africa, strongly rejected by Augustine, whose leadership eventually won the day.

40. The three writings mentioned below, Tertullian's *Apology*, *On Prescription against Heretics*, and *On Baptism* come from his pre-Montanist period. See Alexander Roberts and James Donaldson, eds.,

Anti-Nicene Fathers: Volume 3. Latin Christianity: Its Founder, Tertullian. I Apologetic; II Anti-Marcion; III Ethical (Peabody, MA: Hendrickson, 2004 [reprint of the 1885 edition of the Christian Literature publishing company]), 8–12.

41. Recognized as eucharistic by Bradshaw and Johnson, *Eucharistic Liturgies*, 31–32.

42. Roberts and Donaldson, *Anti-Nicene Fathers*. The translation of *Apology* 39 is found on pp. 46–47.

43. Paul's dealing with the incestuous man in 1 Cor 5:1–8 comes to mind.

44. Roberts and Donaldson, *Anti-Nicene Fathers*, 3:263.

45. See William H. C. Frend, *The Rise of Christianity* (London: Darton, Longman & Todd, 1984), 350–51: Tertullian "could not allow the presence of the impure, the adulterer, and other demon-inspired sinners in its midst, least of all if they had been clergy.... The three capital sins of idolatry, adultery, and bloodshed were 'unpardonable.'"

46. Roberts and Donaldson, *Anti-Nicene Fathers*, 3:679.

47. Ibid., 3:659. See further David Konstan, *Before Forgiveness: The Origins of a Moral Idea* (Cambridge: Cambridge University Press, 2010), 125.

48. See Henri Crouzel, *Origen: The Life and Thought of the First Great Theologian*, trans. A. S. Worrall (San Francisco: Harper & Row, 1989).

49. Ibid., 226.

50. With reference to Rom 14:23.

51. John Patrick, "Origen's Commentary on the Gospel of Matthew," in *Anti-Nicene Fathers: Volume 9. The Gospel of Peter, The Diatesseron of Tatian, The Apocalypse of Peter, The Apocalyses of the Virgin and Sedrach, The Testament of Abraham, The Acts of Xanthippe and Polyxena, The Narrative of Zosimus, The Apology of Aristides, The Epistles of Clement (complete text), Origen's Commentary on John, Books 1-10, and Commentary on Matthew, Books 1, 2, and 10–14*, ed. Alan Menzies (Peabody, MA: Hendrickson, 2004 [reprint of 1896–97 edition of the Christian Literature Publishing Company]), 443.

52. See Crouzel, *Origen*, 228. This position, if it can be called that, distinguishes Origen from Tertullian and the later Donatist crisis.

53. For more detail, see Moloney, *Reading the New Testament in the Church*, 57–63.

54. Philip Schaff, ed., *A Select Library of the Nicene and Post-Nicene*

Fathers of the Christian Church: Volume VII. Augustin: Homilies on the Gospel of John, Homilies on the First Epistle of John, Soliliquies (Grand Rapids: Wm B. Eerdmans, 1978), 312–14.

55. MacCulloch, *A History of Christianity*, 224.

56. Ibid.

57. Joel C. Elowsky, ed., *Commentary on John: Cyril of Alexandria*, trans. David R. Maxwell, Ancient Christian Texts, 2 vols. (Downers Grove, IL: IVP Academic, 2015), 2:129–31.

58. For an introduction to Cyril's rhetorical skills, see Susan Wessel, *Cyril of Alexandria and the Nestorian Controversy: The Making of a Saint and of a Heretic*, Oxford Early Christian Studies (Oxford: Oxford University Press, 2004), 183–89. Wessel comments, "Significant moments of biblical history were reinterpreted in relation to Christ's sacred drama" (p. 189).

59. For the commentary on John 20:17, see Elowsky, *Commentary on John*, 2:360–62. Given the similarity between Augustine and Cyril in their interpretation of John 13:26–27, it is interesting to note that Augustine sees Mary Magdalene as representative of the Gentile world. Once Jesus has ascended to the Father, then he will be universally available "to be touched spiritually" (*Homilies on the Gospel of John* CXXI.3).

60. With reference to Matt 9:13.

61. For a survey of the Church fathers, coming to the same conclusion, see Konstan, *Before Forgiveness*, 125–45. Konstan surveys the apostolic fathers, John Chrysostom, the Cappadocian fathers, Origen, Ephrem, Augustine, and Leo the Great. He argues that the fathers continue biblical traditions by insisting on divine forgiveness offered to the humbly repentant, but say nothing about interpersonal forgiveness. For an even more extensive overview of patristic and later Eastern and monastic texts, see John Chryssavgis, *Repentance and Confession in the Orthodox Church* (Brooklyne, MA: The Holy Cross Orthodox Press, 2004), 19–94.

62. For a critical edition of the two Latin texts, see CCSL, CXXXVIIIA, 359–60, and 403.

63. For a critical edition of the Latin text, see CCSL XCI, 46, and XCIA, 750–51.

64. The Latin (e.g., Leo and Fulgentius) and the Greek (e.g., Athanasius of Alexandria, his successor Cyril, and Maximus) traditions

developed the important theological theme of *theiōsis* ("deification"): the potential of creation to realize its divine finality. See Denis Edwards, *Partaking of God: Trinity, Evolution, and Ecology* (Collegeville, MN: Liturgical Press, 2014), 37–53. I am grateful to my colleague, Dr. Cullen Joyce, for support in accessing Maximus's *Letter* 11.

65. For a remarkable study of a broad cross-section of eastern monastic traditions showing the deep sorrow (*penthos*: heartfelt compunction) that marks the God-given recognition that sin deprives the believer of the complete and utter joy that only God can offer, see Irénée Hausherr, *Penthos: The Doctrine of Compunction in the Christian East*, trans. Anselm Hufstader, Cistercian Studies Series 53 (Kalamazoo, MI: Cistercian Publications, 1982). See also Chryssavgis, *Repentance and Confession*, 9–11.

66. See the moving study of this process, as practiced by Ambrose in Milan, and his convert, Augustine, in Hippo: Garry Wills, *Font of Life: Ambrose, Augustine, and the Mystery of Baptism* (Oxford/New York: Oxford University Press, 2012).

67. Chryssavgis, *Repentance and Confession*, 11–14. The citation is from p. 12.

68. For more detail, See Moloney, *Reading the New Testament*, 1–21.

69. Anyone who has read the novels or watched the filmed versions of Ken Follett's renditions on this period, *Pillars of the Earth* and *World without End*, which focused on the conflict between the Church, the State, and the suffering people trapped in these conflicts, will have some idea why this reform was necessary.

70. See MacCulloch, *A History of Christianity*, 363–95.

71. Interestingly, it was this aspect of twelfth-century Catholicism that led Ken Follett, who had been raised in a Puritan background, to write his two novels that focus on the emergence of Gothic architecture and the context of the rich liturgical settings of Medieval England.

72. The abbreviation DS indicates a fundamental reference work for theologians. First edited by Henry Denzinger, later editions came from Adolf Schönmetzger. It is an invaluable collection of all the major doctrinal and moral teachings of the Catholic Church, set within their origins (e.g., Council of Florence, Council of Trent, First Vatican Council, etc.) across its long history. The numbers given after the sigla

DS are located in the margins. Bibliographical details can be found in the "Abbreviations" found at the beginning of this book.

73. For a balanced assessment of the history and importance of the Council of Trent, see John W. O'Malley, *Trent: What Happened at the Council* (Cambridge, MA: Harvard University Press, 2013).

74. For a very good synthesis, see Oswald Bayer, *Martin Luther's Theology: A Contemporary Interpretation*, trans. Thomas H. Trapp (Grand Rapids: Eerdmans, 2008), 270–73.

75. Cited by Bayer, *Martin Luther's Theology*, 272.

76. Centuries of such abuse is reflected in the contemporary canon law of the Catholic Church. There are no less than 14 canons (canons 945–58) regulating the association of "payment" with the celebration of Masses. See *Code of Canon Law*, 306–9.

77. For a fully documented study that draws these conclusions, see Bradshaw and Johnson, *Eucharistic Liturgies*, 193–231. See the conclusions, summarized above, on pp. 230–31.

78. The 2001 document from the Congregation for Divine Worship and the Discipline of the Sacraments, *Liturgiam Authenticam*, insists on the continued practice of many of these nonbiblical, but very Rome-focused, practices.

79. For a summary and a collection of texts from Augustine, see David G. Hunter, ed., *Marriage in the Early Church*, Sources of Early Christian Thought (Minneapolis: Fortress Press, 1992), 102–27. For a helpful, sympathetic reading of Augustine's teaching on sex and marriage, see Garry Wills, *Augustine*, Penguin Lives Series (New York: Viking Penguin, 1999), 126–45.

80. Peter Lombard's *Sentences* became the standard textbook for Theology at the universities for four centuries. Martin Luther and John Calvin refer to it with respect.

81. On the influence that the *Decree for the Armenians* had on the decision taken at Trent, see O'Malley, *Trent*, 119.

82. A good synthesis of Catholic history can be found in Waldemar Molinski, "Marriage," in *Encyclopedia of Theology*, ed. Karl Rahner, trans. John Griffiths (London: Burns & Oates, 1975), 905–10.

83. In the so-called Western Schism, popes in Avignon, Rome, and even Spain claimed the Petrine office. At one stage, there were three claimants to the papal throne. The previously mentioned councils debated the question unsuccessfully, until a "winner" emerged from

the Council of Constance, and the Roman papacy was definitively established at the Fifth Lateran Council. Most historians see this as the beginning of the eventual definition of papal infallibility at the First Vatican Council in 1870. *Conciliarism* was the term given to a movement that tried, through the previously mentioned councils, to establish that an Ecumenical Council had authority over the papacy. The definitive work on this period is Brian Tierney, *Religion, Law and the Growth of Constitutional Thought 1150–1650* (Cambridge: Cambridge University Press, 1982). For a lively account of the period, see MacCulloch, *A History of Christianity*, 551–603.

CHAPTER 4

1. As reported in Joshua J. McElwee, "Catholicism Can and Must Change, Francis Forcefully Tells Italian Church Gathering," *National Catholic Reporter*, November 10, 2015, https://www.ncronline.org/news/vatican/catholicism-can-and-must-change-francis-forcefully-tells-italian-church-gathering.

2. Pope Francis, "Catholicism Can and Must Change," 4. See similar sentiments from Pope Francis in *Amoris Laetitia* 108, 297, 308, etc.

3. Pope Francis, "Catholicism Can and Must Change," 4–5.

4. We do not have any further information, as the brief Letter to the Galatians stands alone. We do not know whether or not Paul's passionate intervention resolved the problem in Galatia.

5. For a survey of this discussion and a sound defense of the literary and theological unity of 2 Corinthians, see Frank J. Matera, *II Corinthians: A Commentary*, The New Testament Library (Louisville: Westminster John Knox, 2003), 24–32.

6. For a very helpful guide to the Church at Corinth, see Jerome Murphy-O'Connor, *Saint Paul's Corinth: Texts and Archaeology*, Good News Studies 6 (Wilmington, DE: Michael Glazier, 1983).

7. See Moloney, *A Body Broken*, 51–57.

8. This could be said for all of the genuine Pauline Letters, but it is especially true in the Corinthian correspondence, as he goes back and forth with them over many issues, including his own authority as an Apostle in 2 Corinthians. See Edsall, *Paul's Witness*, 59, for a summary.

9. For a summary of this, see Moloney, *The Resurrection of the Messiah*, 137–82.

10. The sacrament of reconciliation has its own unique history in the Western Church, from the problem of postbaptismal sin in the earliest decades, into major public penitential practices, until the Irish practice of oral confession was gradually introduced by the Irish monks in their missionary activities in Europe. It was canonized at the Council of Trent. A sure guide is the classical study of Bernhard Poschmann, *Penance and Anointing of the Sick*, The Herder History of Dogma (Freiburg/London: Herder/Burns & Oates, 1964), 1–209.

11. For a stimulating reflection on the Creed, see Anthony J. Kelly, *The Creed by Heart: Re-Learning the Nicene Creed* (Blackburn: Harper Collins, 1996). On the above introductory reflections, see pp. 1–13. For the original Greek and a Latin translation of the Creed, see DS 150.

12. For further reflection on the danger of distorting traditions, see Moloney, *Reading the New Testament in the Church*, 191–201.

13. Kelly, *Creed by Heart*, 8–9.

14. Kelly, *Creed by Heart*, 24.

15. The evocative power of these words of Jesus from the Gospel of John is shown at all major sporting events in the United States. Someone will inevitably raise a banner, bearing simply "John 3:16." Everyone present is aware of what is being proclaimed.

16. The language of Rom 3:21–26, and elsewhere in the New Testament, conjures up an image of God's "buying back" the sinner (from Satan?) through a bloody sacrifice. This is not the message of the New Testament, despite its occasional appearance. Such imagery has its roots in redemptive blood sacrifices of the Old Testament. It has been transformed by the God loving gift of his Son (see, e.g., Heb 9:23–28). For a fine contemporary treatment of this question, see Ingolf E. Dalferth, *Crucified and Risen: Restructuring the Grammar of Christology*, trans. Jo Bennett (Grand Rapids: Baker Academic, 2015), 235–313. See the helpful, simple presentation of this, explaining the Christian transformation of the Old Testament background of blood sacrifices in Patrick J. Flanagan, *Just What Is Sacrifice? An Exploration of the Sacrifice of Christ and Our Sharing of That Sacrifice in the Eucharist: Questions and Answers* (Strathfield: St Pauls Publications, 2016), 47–64.

17. See Moloney, *Love in the Gospel of John*.

18. Two thousand years of theological and christological reflection, guided by the great councils, have sought to articulate how this mystery can be best explained. For an impressive recent study, see Dalferth, *Crucified and Risen*. As Kelly, *Creed by Heart*, 13, notes, "Our profession of faith operates in a field of meaning that can never be fully articulated."

19. History has not served confirmation well. Originally associated with the ritual of baptism, imparting the life of the Spirit at that moment, once the "timing" of the conferral of the sacrament was separated (as a result of the possibility that anyone can administer baptism, but not confirmation), it is now regularly associated with a step into mature Christianity. Although helpful, this was not the original role of the sacrament.

20. For this interpretation of John 19:25–35, see Francis J. Moloney, *The Gospel of John*, Sacra Pagina 4 (Collegeville, MN: Liturgical Press, 1998), 502–10.

21. Too often reflection on the saving action of God in and through Jesus Christ is limited to his death and resurrection. This must be completed by reflection on the ascension and the gift of the Spirit that renders present the divine work among us. See the important study of Anthony J. Kelly, *Upward: Faith, Church, and the Ascension of Christ* (Collegeville, MN: Liturgical Press, 2014).

22. Citing the *Exsultet* from the Easter Vigil (and the biblical readings from the Easter Vigil) calls on an ancient theological principle: what the Church prays, the Church believes (*lex orandi, lex credendi*). The use of this remarkable Easter hymn/acclamation was an ancient practice in Italy, Gaul, Spain, and Africa (see Augustine, *De Civitate Dei*, XV.22). Its introduction in Rome is associated with Pope Zosimus (417–18).

23. Schaff, *Nicene and Post-Nicene Fathers*, 7:350.

24. Kelly, *Creed by Heart*, 189.

25. Konstan, *Before Forgiveness*, 91–145. Konstan's fascinating study correctly argues that the introduction of the divine as an agent of forgiveness determines this novelty. His main claim is that interpersonal forgiveness does not emerge until the eighteenth and nineteenth centuries, when the Christian concept of forgiveness is secularized (see pp. 146–71). His intense focus on "forgiveness" vocabulary perhaps leads to a lack of appreciation of the interpersonal forgiveness that

flows from the early Christian command to mutual love. I miss reference to Rodney Stark's *Sociology of Early Christianity.*

26. John Chryssavgis, *Repentance and Confession in the Orthodox Church* (Brooklyne, MA: The Holy Cross Orthodox Press, 2004), 4, 14.

27. I am grateful to my colleague Christiaan Jacobs-Vandergeer, who suggested that I add this important qualification.

28. Pope Francis made obvious his care for Catholic marriages in difficulty in his *motu proprio* (a statement that comes from his own perspective as pope) *Mitis Iudex Dominus Iesus*, published on September 8, 2015. He has radically eased the conditions (and the costs) of the process of the "annulment" of a marriage in the Catholic Tradition. For a clear explanation of the new canonical process, see Albert McDonnell, "Mercy Applied: Marriage Annulments," *The Furrow* 67 (2016): 92–97.

29. Moloney, *A Body Broken*. On the contemporary dilemma in today's Church and world, see pp. 13–39, and for a biblical, theological, and pastoral reflection on divorce, remarriage, and the Eucharist, see pp. 205–54.

30. See Pope Francis, *Amoris Laetitia*, 71–75, for a rich presentation of the traditional Catholic understanding of the sacrament of marriage.

31. Forkman, *The Limits of Religious Community*, 217, concludes his comprehensive study of this question by claiming that neither Jesus nor the early Church saw the holiness of the community as the important issue. It was "the individual's standpoint in face of the message about the kingdom of God."

32. Patrick Considine, "Remarriage and the Eucharist," *Priest and People* 3 (1989): 226–27.

33. Words from Gilbert Keith Chesterton's *Orthodoxy* (New York: Doubleday, 1959), 100, come to mind: "The church announces terrible ideas and devouring doctrines, each one of them strong enough to turn into a false religion and lay waste the world.... Thus, if some small mistake is made in doctrine, huge blunders may be made in human happiness."

34. Pope Francis, "Catholicism Can and Must Change," 5.

35. Figure from Ruth Weston and Livia Qu, "Working Out Relationships," *Australian Family Trends* 3 (Australian Institute of

Family Studies, 2013), https://aifs.gov.au/publications/working-out-relationships.

36. Pope Francis, *Amoris Laetitia*, 300, does state the possibility of "a responsible personal and pastoral decision in particular cases," devoting attention to the principle that "the degree of responsibility is not equal in all cases." This does not mean recourse to "internal forum," but rather the establishment of a pastoral process like that suggested below.

37. *Amoris Laetitia* 300n336.

38. Despite the crushing evidence of a Church leadership that refused to accept any responsibility for countless episodes of the abuse of minors in all parts of the world, there are still cardinals, bishops, and priests who refuse to accept that they have betrayed their mission as bearers of God's saving love in the world. They are often the same individuals who reject a rethinking of any Tridentine "doctrine." On this, see the important study of Marie Keenan, *Child Sexual Abuse & The Catholic Church: Gender, Power, and Organizational Culture* (Oxford/New York: Oxford University Press, 2012), especially pp. 230–82.

39. See, for example, Jean Vanier, *From Brokenness to Community: The Wit Lectures. Harvard University, the Divinity School* (New York: Paulist Press, 1992); Anthony J. Kelly, *God is Love: The Heart of Christian Faith* (Collegeville, MN: Liturgical Press, 2012), 78–94.

40. Chryssavgis, *Repentance and Forgiveness*, 9–10.

BIBLIOGRAPHY

Allison, Dale C., Jr. *Constructing Jesus: Memory, Imagination and History*. Grand Rapids: Baker Academic, 2010.

Attridge, Harold W. *The Epistle to the Hebrews*. Hermeneia. Philadelphia: Fortress Press, 1989.

Barnard, Leslie William. *St. Justin Martyr the First and Second Apologies*. Ancient Christian Writers 56. New York: Paulist Press, 1997.

Barrett, C. Kingsley. *The First Epistle to the Corinthians*. Black's New Testament Commentaries. London: A. & C. Black, 1971.

———. *The Gospel according to John*. 2nd ed. London: SPCK, 1978.

Bayer, Oswald. *Martin Luther's Theology: A Contemporary Interpretation*. Translated by Thomas H. Trapp. Grand Rapids: Eerdmans, 2008.

Bernard, John H. *A Critical and Exegetical Commentary on the Gospel of John*. International Critical Commentary. Edinburgh: T. & T. Clark, 1928.

Bornkamm, Günther. "Lord's Supper and Church in Paul." In *Early Christian Experience*, translated by Paul L. Hammer, 123–60. London: SCM Press, 1963.

Bradshaw, Paul F., and Maxwell Johnson. *The Eucharistic Liturgies: Their Evolution and Interpretation*. Alcuin Club Collections 87. London: SPCK, 2012.

Brown, Raymond E. *An Introduction to the New Testament*. The Anchor Bible Reference Library. New York: Doubleday, 1997.

Brown, Sherri. *Gift upon Gift: Covenant through Word in the Gospel of John*. Princeton Theological Monograph Series 144. Eugene, OR: Pickwick Publications, 2010.

Byrne, Brendan J. *Paul and the Christian Woman*. Homebush: St Pauls Publications, 1988.

———. *Reckoning with Romans: A Contemporary Reading of Paul's Gospel*. Good News Studies 18. Wilmington, DE: Michael Glazier, 1986.

Canon Law Society of America. *Code of Canon Law: Latin-English Edition*. Washington, DC: Canon Law Society of America, 1999.

Catechism of the Catholic Church. Homebush: St Pauls Publications, 1994.

Charlesworth, James H., ed. *The Old Testament Pseudepigrapha*. 2 vols. London: Darton, Longman & Todd, 1983.

Chenderlin, Fritz. *"Do This as My Memorial": The Semantic and Conceptual Background and Value of Anamnēsis in 1 Corinthians 11:24–25*. Analecta Biblica 99. Rome: Biblical Institute Press, 1982.

Chesterton, Gilbert Keith. *Orthodoxy*. New York: Doubleday, 1959.

Chryssavgis, John. *Repentance and Confession in the Orthodox Church*. Brooklyne, MA: The Holy Cross Orthodox Press, 2004.

Collins, Raymond N. *First Corinthians*. Sacra Pagina 7. Collegeville, MN: Liturgical Press, 1999.

Congregation for Divine Worship and the Discipline of the Sacraments. *Liturgiam Authenticam: On the Use of the Vernacular Languages in the Publication of the Books of the Roman Liturgy*. Vatican City: Editrice Libreria Vaticana, 2001.

Considine, Patrick. "Remarriage and the Eucharist." *Priest and People* 3 (1989): 226–27.

Conzelmann, Hans. *1 Corinthians: A Commentary on the First Epistle to the Corinthians*. Translated by James W. Leitch. Hermeneia. Philadelphia: Fortress, 1988.

Crouzel, Henri. *Origen: The Life and Thought of the First Great Theologian*. Translated by A. S. Worrall. San Francisco: Harper & Row, 1989.

Culpepper, R. Alan. "The Johannine *Hypodeigma*: A Reading of John 13:1–38." *Semeia* 53 (1991): 133–52.

Dahl, Nils A. "Anamnesis: Memory and Commemoration in Early Christianity." In *Jesus in the Memory of the Early Church*, 11–29. Minneapolis: Augsburg, 1976.

Dalferth, Ingolf E. *Crucified and Risen: Restructuring the Grammar of Christology*. Translated by Jo Bennett. Grand Rapids, MI: Baker Academic, 2015.

Daly, Robert J. "From the New Testament to the Liturgies of the Golden Age." *Theological Studies* 68 (2007): 3–22.

Davies, William D., and Dale C. Allison Jr. *A Critical and Exegetical Commentary on the Gospel of Matthew*. International Critical Commentary. 3 vols. Edinburgh: T. & T. Clark, 1988–97.

Dequeker, Luc, and Willem Zuidema. "The Eucharist and St. Paul: 1 Cor. 11.17–34." *Concilium* 4 (1968): 26–31.

Edsall, Benjamin A. *Paul's Witness to Formative Early Christian Instruction*. Wissenschaftliche Untersuchungen zum Neuen Testament 2.365. Tübingen: Mohr Siebeck, 2014.

Edwards, Denis. *Partaking of God: Trinity, Evolution, and Ecology*. Collegeville, MN: Liturgical Press, 2014.

Elowsky, Joel C., ed. *Commentary on John: Cyril of Alexandria*. Translated by David R. Maxwell. Ancient Christian Texts. 2 vols. Downers Grove: IVP Academic, 2015.

Fitzmyer, Joseph A. *First Corinthians*. The Anchor Yale Bible 32. New Haven: Yale University Press, 2008.

Flanagan, Patrick J. *Just What is Sacrifice? An Exploration of the Sacrifice of Christ and Our Sharing of That Sacrifice in the Eucharist: Questions and Answers*. Strathfield: St Pauls Publications, 2016.

Forkman, Göran. *The Limits of Religious Community: Expulsion from the Religious Community within the Qumran Sect, within Rabbinic Judaism, and within Primitive Christianity*. Translated by Pearl Sjölander. Coniectanea Biblica New Testament Series 5. Lund: Gleerup, 1972.

Fotopoulos, John. *Food Offered to Idols in Roman Corinth: A Social-Rhetorical Reconsideration of 1 Corinthians 8:1—11:1*. Wissenschaftliche Untersuchungen zum Neuen Testament 2.151. Tübingen: Mohr Siebeck, 2003.

Francis, Pope. "Catholicism Can and Must Change, Francis Forcefully Tells Italian Church Gathering." Online at https://www.ncronline.org/news/vatican/catholicism-can-and-must-change-francis-forcefully-tells-italian-church-gathering.

———. *Post-Synodal Exhortation Amoris Laetitia* (Vatican City: Editrice Vaticana, 2016).

Frend, William H. C. *The Rise of Christianity*. London: Darton, Longman & Todd, 1984.

Gaventa, Beverley. "'You Proclaim the Lord's Death': 1 Corinthians 11:26 and Paul's Understanding of Worship." *Review and Expositor* 80 (1983): 377–87.

Hamman, Adalbert, and Mario Maritano. "Eucharist." In *Encyclopedia of Ancient Christianity Produced by the Institutum Patristicum*

Augustinianum, 1:854–57. 3 vols. Downers Grove, IL: IVP Academic, 2014.

Hausherr, Irénée. *Penthos: The Doctrine of Compunction in the Christian East*. Translated by Anselm Hufstader, Cistercian Studies Series 53. Kalamazoo, MI: Cistercian Publications, 1982.

Henrici, Peter. "'Do This in Remembrance of Me': The Sacrifice of Christ and the Sacrifice of the Faithful." *Communio: International Catholic Review* 12 (1985): 146–57.

Holmes, Michael W. *The Apostolic Fathers: Greek Texts and English Translation*. 3rd ed. Grand Rapids, MI: Baker Academic, 2007.

Hunter, David G. *Marriage in the Early Church*. Sources of Early Christian Thought. Minneapolis: Fortress Press, 1992.

Johnson, Luke T. *The Gospel of Luke*. Sacra Pagina 3. Collegeville, MN: Liturgical Press, 1991.

———. *Hebrews: A Commentary*. The New Testament Library. Louisville, KY: Westminster John Knox, 2006.

Karris, Robert. *Luke: Artist and Theologian: Luke's Passion Account as Literature*. New York: Paulist Press, 1985.

Keenan, Marie. *Child Sexual Abuse & The Catholic Church: Gender, Power, and Organizational Culture*. Oxford/New York: Oxford University Press, 2012.

Kelly, Anthony J. *The Creed by Heart: Re-Learning the Nicene Creed*. Blackburn: Harper Collins, 1996.

———. *God Is Love: The Heart of Christian Faith*. Collegeville, MN: Liturgical Press, 2012.

———. *Upward: Faith, Church, and the Ascension of Christ*. Collegeville, MN: Liturgical Press, 2014.

Kloppenborg, John S. *Q, The Earliest Gospels: An Introduction to the Original Stories and Sayings of Jesus*. Louisville, KY: Westminster John Knox, 2008.

Kodell, Jerome. *The Eucharist in the New Testament*. Zacchaeus Studies New Testament. Wilmington, DE: Michael Glazier, 1989.

Koester, Craig R. *Hebrews*. The Anchor Bible 36. New York: Doubleday, 2001.

Konstan, David. *Before Forgiveness: The Origins of a Moral Idea*. Cambridge: Cambridge University Press, 2010.

Lane, William L. *Hebrews*. Word Biblical Commentary 47. 2 vols. Nashville: Thomas Nelson, 1991.

Léon-Dufour, Xavier. *Sharing the Eucharistic Bread: The Witness of the New Testament*. Translated by Matthew J. O'Connell. New York: Paulist Press, 1997.

Luz, Ulrich. *Matthew*. Translated by James E. Crowe. Hermeneia. 3 vols. Minneapolis: Fortress, 2001–7.

MacCulloch, Diarmaid. *A History of Christianity: The First Three Thousand Years*. London: Allen Lane, 2009.

Martyn, J. Louis. *History and Theology in the Fourth Gospel*. The New Testament Library. 3rd ed. Louisville, KY: Westminster John Knox, 2003.

Matera, Frank. *II Corinthians: A Commentary*. The New Testament Library. Louisville, KY: Westminster John Knox, 2003.

McDonnell, Albert. "Mercy Applied: Marriage Annulments." *The Furrow* 67 (2016): 92–97.

McGowan, Andrew B. "The Meals of Jesus and the Meals of the Church: Eucharistic Origins and the Admission to Communion." In *Studia Liturgica Diversa: Essays in Honor of Paul F. Bradshaw*, edited by Maxwell E. Johnson and L. Edward Phillips, 101–15. Portland, OR: Pastoral Press, 2004.

Minear, Paul S. "Some Glimpses of Luke's Sacramental Theology." *Worship* 44 (1970): 322–31.

Molinski, Waldemar. "Marriage." In *Encyclopedia of Theology*, edited by Karl Rahner, 905–10. Translated by John Griffiths. London: Burns & Oates, 1975.

Moloney, Francis J. *A Body Broken for a Broken People: Marriage, Divorce, and the Eucharist*. New York: Paulist Press, 2016.

———. *The Gospel of John*. Sacra Pagina 4. Collegeville, MN: Liturgical Press, 1998.

———. *The Gospel of Mark: A Commentary*. Grand Rapids, MI: Baker Academic, 2012.

———. "The Literary Unity of John 13,1–38." *Ephemerides Theologicae Lovanienses* 91 (2015): 33–53.

———. *Love in the Gospel of John: An Exegetical, Theological, and Literary Study*. Grand Rapids: Baker Academic, 2013.

———. *Reading the New Testament in the Church: A Primer for Pastors, Religious Educators, and Believers*. Grand Rapids: Baker Academic, 2015.

———. *The Resurrection of the Messiah: A Narrative Commentary on the Resurrection Accounts in the Four Gospels*. New York: Paulist Press, 2013.

———. "Synchronic Interpretation." 2 vols. In *The Oxford Encyclopedia of Biblical Interpretation*, 2:345–54. Oxford: Oxford University Press, 2013.

Murphy-O'Connor, Jerome. "Eucharist and Community in First Corinthians." *Worship* 50 (1976): 370–85; 51 (1977): 56–69.

———. *1 Corinthians*. New Testament Message 10. Wilmington, DE: Michael Glazier, 1979.

———. *Saint Paul's Corinth: Texts and Archaeology*. Good News Studies 6. Wilmington, DE: Michael Glazier, 1983.

Nestle-Aland, *Novum Testamentum Graece. Greek-English New Testament*. 28th ed. Stuttgart: Deutsche Bibelgesellschaft, 2013.

Neyrey, Jerome. *The Passion According to Luke: A Redaction Study of Luke's Soteriology*. New York: Paulist Press, 1985.

O'Malley, John W. *Trent: What Happened at the Council*. Cambridge, MA: Harvard University Press, 2013.

Patrick, John. "Origen's Commentary on the Gospel of Matthew." In *Anti-Nicene Fathers: Volume 9: The Gospel of Peter, The Diatesseron of Tatian, the Apocalypse of Peter, The Apocalypses of the Virgen and Sedrach, The Testament of Abraham, The Acts of Xanthippe and Polyxena, The Narrative of Zosimus, The Apology of Aristides, The Epistles of Clement (complete text), Origen's Commentary on John, Books 1–10, and Commentary on Matthew, Books 1, 2, and 10–14*, edited by Alan Menzies, 411–512. Peabody: Hendrickson, 2004. Reprint of the 1896–97 edition of the Christian Literature Publishing Company.

Perkins, Pheme. *First Corinthians*. Paideia Commentaries on the New Testament. Grand Rapids, MI: Baker Academic, 2012.

Piolanti, Antonio. *The Holy Eucharist*. New York: Desclée, 1961.

Pitre, Brad. *Jesus and the Last Supper*. Grand Rapids, MI: Eerdmans, 2015.

Poschmann, Bernard. *Penance and Anointing of the Sick*. The Herder History of Dogma. Freiburg/London: Herder/Burns & Oates, 1964.

Ratzinger, Joseph. "Sacred Scripture in the Life of the Church." In *Commentary on the Documents of Vatican II*, edited by Herbert

Vorgrimler, 3:262–72. 5 vols. London: Burns & Oates/Herder & Herder, 1969.

Roberts, Alexander, and James Donaldson, eds. *Anti-Nicene Fathers: Volume 3. Latin Christianity: Its Founder Tertullian. 1 Apologetic; II Anti-Marcion; III Ethical.* Peabody, MA: Hendrickson, 2004. Reprint of the 1985 edition of the Christian Literature Publishing Company.

Schaff, Philip, ed. *A Select Library of the Nicene and Post-Nicene Fathers of the Christian Church: Volume VII. Augustin: Homilies on the Gospel of John, Homilies on the First Epistle of John, Soliliquies.* Grand Rapids, MI: Wm. B. Eerdmans, 1978.

Schoedel, William R. *Ignatius of Antioch: A Commentary on the Letters of Ignatius.* Hermeneia. Philadelphia: Fortress Press, 1985.

Shepherd, Tom. "The Narrative Function of Markan Intercalation." *New Testament Studies* 41 (1995): 522–40.

Stark, Rodney. *The Rise of Christianity.* Princeton: Princeton University Press, 1996.

Taft, Robert F. "Mass without the Consecration? The Historical Agreement on the Eucharist between the Catholic Church and the Assyrian Churches of the East, Promulgated 26 October, 2001." *Worship* 77 (2003): 482–509.

Tannehill, Robert C. *The Narrative Unity of Luke-Acts: A Literary Interpretation.* 2 vols. Philadelphia: Fortress Press, 1991.

Theissen, Gerd. "Social Integration and Sacramental Activity: An Analysis of 1 Cor 11:17–34." In *The Social Setting of Pauline Christianity: Essays on Corinth,* 145–74. Philadelphia: Fortress Press, 1982.

Thompson, James W. *Hebrews.* Paideia Commentaries on the New Testament. Grand Rapids, MI: Baker Academic, 2008.

Tierney, Brian. *Religion, Law and the Growth of Constitutional Thought 1150–1650.* Cambridge: Cambridge University Press, 1982.

Vanier, Jean. *From Brokenness to Community: The Wit Lectures. Harvard University, the Divinity School.* Mahwah, NJ: Paulist Press, 1992.

Wessel, Susan. *Cyril of Alexandria and the Nestorian Controversy: The Masking of a Saint and of a Heretic.* Oxford Early Christian Studies. Oxford: Oxford University Press, 2004.

Westcott, Brooke W. *The Epistle to the Hebrews: The Greek Text with Notes and Essays.* London: Macmillan, 1889.

Weston, Ruth, and Livia Qu. "Working Out Relationships." *Australian Family Trends* 3 (Australian Institute of Family Studies). Online at https://aifs.gov.au/publications/working-out-relationships.

Wills, Garry. *Augustine*. Penguin Lives Series. New York: Viking Penguin, 1999.

———. *Font of Life: Ambrose, Augustine, and the Mystery of Baptism*. Oxford/New York: Oxford University Press, 2012.

Index of Authors